CW01513297

NORTHBOUND ON THE WEST HIGHLAND WAY

Paul Amess

Kingstown Publishing

Contents

Preface

Let's get one thing straight right from the start: I am not Bear Grylls. I don't drink from streams with a straw made of moss, I don't eat squirrels I've personally wrestled out of a tree, and if I ever ended up sleeping inside the carcass of a freshly deceased animal, it would be because I mistook it for a Travelodge.

What follows is the story of me, an allegedly grown adult with the knees of a pensioner and the optimism of someone who's clearly not read the weather forecast, attempting to walk the West Highland Way. That's 96 miles of Scotland's finest scenery, which would be great if you could actually see it through the horizontal rain and face-slapping midges.

Along the way, I encountered stunning lochs, towering Munros, ancient battlefields, and the kind of public toilets that haunt your dreams. I learned important lessons like: waterproof trousers are a lie, walking poles are not a sign of weakness, and if you ever hear someone shout "just a wee incline" you should punch them immediately.

This book is not a guide. If you're looking for practical advice, turn back now. Honestly, turn back. There's still time. But if you fancy joining me for a slightly damp, occasionally sweary, historically confused ramble through one of the most beautiful parts of the UK - while laughing at my suffering - then you're in exactly the right place.

So lace up your boots, grab a snack (you'll need it), and prepare to experience the Scottish Highlands the way they were meant to be seen: through eyes blurred with regret and rain.

Let the trudge begin.

The West Highland Way

The mountains are calling, and I must go.
John Muir

The West Highland Way had been calling me for years, like some persistent drunk at a karaoke night who refuses to believe *Sweet Caroline* has ended. But, thanks to a few minor inconveniences —such as having to earn a living, feed the children, and pretend to be a responsible adult—I'd never quite managed to get up there and do it.

But that had changed now. The stars had aligned, the kids had finally stopped demanding meals every five minutes, and Robin, Chris and I —clearly operating on some kind of frostbitten brainwave—had made the decision in the middle of winter, as snow blanketed everything in sight, that we were off. As soon as spring arrived, and as soon as lockdown ended, we were going to walk the West Highland Way. The children could fend for themselves. They'd seen *Bear Grylls*. They'd be fine.

My wife didn't even look all that fussed about

me vanishing, which was either a touching display of confidence in my survival skills or a cry for help. I suspect she was secretly overjoyed at the prospect of a peaceful, tidy house, and possibly hoped I'd stay lost in the Highlands permanently. She even told me there's "no point in you being around during the holidays anyway, you never listen." Which, frankly, is outrageous. I protested my innocence, of course, only to be reminded of a very specific incident where she nudged me mid-conversation and accused me of not listening. I apparently replied, "That's a weird way to start a conversation." Which, in fairness, is objectively hilarious and should've earned me a round of applause, not an argument.

We weren't exactly going to have the place to ourselves, mind you. Every year, around thirty thousand people slog their way along the entire route, presumably under the illusion that it'll be a fun and scenic adventure rather than a multi-day test of willpower, waterproofs, and knee cartilage. I often wondered how the so-called 'powers that be' even knew this number. I can only assume there's some poor sod stationed at the end in Fort William, clipboard in hand, counting every dishevelled hiker as they collapse across the finish line looking like survivors of a very polite, very damp apocalypse.

And yes, I say Fort William because that's where it *ends*. You're supposed to walk the route from south to north. That's the official way. The Proper Way. The One True Path. Of course, you *can* walk it the other way, if you enjoy going against the grain and being glared at by every single walker doing it the right way. Nothing says "social pariah" quite like making other people repeatedly stand aside on a narrow trail while you puff past them with the smugness of a man reading the map upside down.

Anyway. The West Highland Way is no spring chicken. It celebrated its 40th birthday on 6th October 2020—which is adorable, if you like long walks and midlife crises. It was born in 1980 thanks to a Glaswegian hero called Tom Hunter, who spent six years of his life getting it all sorted, presumably fuelled by Irn-Bru and sheer bloody-mindedness. It became Scotland's first official long-distance footpath and, like most birthdays during the pandemic, its celebration was a bit... well, naff. With no one allowed out to neck pints and shout about it in person, the poor souls in charge had to throw a virtual party online. Which, to be fair, was surprisingly decent—if you're into that sort of thing. Personally, I miss the days when a celebration meant cake, not a Zoom call and someone forgetting they're on mute.

One of the loudest cheerleaders for the West Highland Way—at least online—is a chap called Jimmie MacGregor. Glaswegian, naturally. Now, if that name doesn't ring a bell, don't worry. He's a folk-singer-turned-TV-presenter who quickly discovered that going outside occasionally is good for you, and he's been banging on about it ever since. He even wrote one of the earlier books about the route, which—annoyingly—is actually very good.

Even if you've never heard of him, odds are you've heard one of his songs at some point, because the man's knocked out over twenty albums. The one I always think of is *Football Crazy*, which he performed with his musical partner Robin Hall—a duo who sound less like musicians and more like the kind of blokes who'd fix your roof for cash-in-hand and a pint. Jimmie's retired now, of course, but he still pops up in the odd promotional video for the trail, including one where he says he's now ninety. Ninety! And yet, bizarrely, he doesn't look a day over eighty-nine. Must be all that fresh air and yodelling.

Now, when it came to actually *getting* to the West Highland Way, things weren't exactly straightforward. Thanks to the pandemic, the rules about what you could do, where you could go, and who you could breathe near had become more complicated than assembling flat-pack furniture with missing instructions and three extra screws.

England—where I live, because I enjoy drizzle and disappointment—had one set of rules. Scotland, being Scotland, had a completely different set, just to keep things spicy. Trying to navigate the differences was like trying to play a board game where nobody actually agrees on the rules, but everyone still insists they're winning.

And yes, I know I said "countries", plural, but let's be honest—Scotland's only a "country" if you're Scottish. In which case, (a) calm down, I'm joking, and (b) that's an excellent sense of humour you've got there. Hold on to it. You're going to need it.

Thankfully, no passport was required for crossing this most turbulent of borders—which was just as well, as international travel was still looking about as likely as a warm day in Fort William. At the time I started scribbling this down—or, more accurately, typing half-thoughts into a phone with thumbs that seemed too fat for modern technology—nobody was going anywhere. Not abroad, not far, not even to the loo without checking the latest government update.

Still, there were encouraging signs. Infections were down, deaths were down, general misery was... well, still quite high, but at least the graphs were pointing in the right direction. Unfortunately, another thing that was constantly coming down was the bloody rain. Honestly, I'm not sure it *stopped* raining that entire spring. It was like the weather had entered a deeply emotional phase and just needed to cry it out over northern Britain.

I'd started doing practice walks, partly to get in

shape for the big adventure, and partly to escape the house without anyone demanding snacks, Wi-Fi passwords or explanations about long division. After a year of lockdown and comfort eating like I was training for the Bake Off *and* a sumo tournament, my fitness levels were somewhere between "could probably manage the stairs" and "might wheeze opening the biscuit tin."

One day, however, I managed to burn over 2,000 calories. I was thrilled—although technically this was just because I burnt a cake that I'd left in the oven.

Still, these sodden, windswept training walks felt like good prep for Scotland, land of soggy boots and regret. I often chuckled to myself as water trickled down the back of my neck, thinking, "Yes, this is definitely character-building. Or trench-foot-building. One of the two."

Eventually, I ran out of places near my house to stomp around. After a year of looping the same dull routes like a confused postman, I'd seen every tree, pylon and angry dog within a ten-mile radius. So, I started venturing further afield in search of something—*anything*—resembling a hill. Sadly, where I live is flatter than a pancake that's been sat on by a lorry, so the options were... limited.

I'd have settled for a gentle incline. A hump. Even a particularly aggressive speed bump. But no—every path was flatter than my enthusiasm for Zoom quizzes. Occasionally I'd find what I generously referred to as a "hill," but it was usually more of a minor swelling in the landscape, the sort of thing a mole might struggle over.

I'd trudge up these pathetic mounds with a heroic sense of purpose, pretending they were training for Ben Nevis. Sometimes I reached the top in under a minute, which should tell you everything you need to know about the *scale* of these majestic peaks. They weren't exactly preparing me for mountainous terrain—but they did wonders for my ego. I'd stand at the top, panting slightly, surveying the car park below like I'd just summited Everest.

Spoiler alert: I had not.

Throughout the past year, the three of us—Robin, Chris and yours truly—had stayed in touch, mainly through messages, occasional video calls, and the odd meme that involved cats swearing. But we hadn't *seen* each other properly in ages, and we definitely hadn't done any walking together, which used to be our version of socialising. You know, the usual: putting one foot in front of the other, getting lost, moaning about blisters, and wondering why we didn't just stay at home with a pint.

Robin and I had managed the odd socially distanced stroll—two men awkwardly shouting at each other across a windy field while trying to remember if 1.5 metres was "about a sheep" or "roughly the length of Boris Johnson's credibility." But I hadn't seen Chris in months, and I found myself genuinely looking forward to it. Mostly for the company. Partly for the fresh air. And just a little bit for the chance that we might get arrested for loitering suspiciously in waterproofs.

You see, proper friendship is forged not in polite dinner parties or wholesome shared interests, but in chaos. Our trio had always bonded over sarcasm, inappropriateness, mild danger, and alcohol consumed in questionable locations. If you can't rely on your mates to lead you up a hill, into a bog, and possibly into a warning from the local constabulary, are they even *really* your mates?

Of course, everyone had an opinion on what was going on. Some people thought lockdowns were vital. Others thought they were a plot by the lizard people to stop us going to Greggs. Personally, like most people, I just sort of went with it—half following the rules, half wondering if the rules had been written by a caffeinated octopus.

Now, I didn't agree with *everything* the powers-that-be imposed on us from their ivory towers— or probably more accurately, their converted home offices with terrible Wi-Fi—but I had skin in the game. My son is immunocompromised, which is a polite way of saying his immune system has all the defensive capabilities of a wet paper bag. So his mum and I figured it was probably wise to play it safe. You know, stay in, mask up, wash our hands like we were about to perform surgery on the Queen.

That said, I watched people behaving in all sorts of interesting ways—from neighbours holding birthday parties with "just a few" hundred guests, to people on the news being fined for driving 200 miles to have a picnic in the Lake District, which is arguably the most British crime imaginable. I didn't always agree with the idiocy, but I could *kind of* understand it. We were all going stir-crazy, stuck in our houses, slowly becoming one with the sofa.

And let's be honest—governing during all of this must've been like trying to herd cats on roller skates. No easy answers. Just a lot of shouting, graphs, and someone somewhere inevitably licking a lamppost.

One thing I did have over a lot of people, though, was experience. I mentioned earlier that my son is immunocompromised—well, that's because he had a liver transplant a few years back, after a cancer diagnosis that turned our lives upside down and then cheerfully drop-kicked the furniture for good measure. He spent months in hospital, and I was the one who stayed with him. Just me, him, and a small sterile room roughly the size of a prison cell, but with slightly worse catering.

Because he had to be kept in isolation, both before and after the transplant—not to mention during chemo—we became accidental pioneers of digital communication. Back then, video calling wasn't something people did unless they were trying to reach a hostage in a Liam Neeson film. But we made it work. He couldn't see his brothers, grandparents or even a cat unless it was on a screen, so we became Zoom ninjas before it was fashionable.

And honestly? That whole experience gave us a weird advantage when the COVID lockdown hit. While others were trying to figure out how to unmute themselves on calls and discovering that their kids are actual goblins when trapped indoors, we were already old hands at the whole isolation thing. We didn't love it—but we managed. No major breakdowns, no interpretive dance videos, no impulse purchases of indoor trampolines. Just a quiet acceptance of the madness, and the occasional passive-aggressive comment about who'd finished the biscuits.

So, with the worst behind us and a national obsession with banana bread slowly dying off, I was finally ready to get back outdoors. I spent most of spring sorting out my camping and walking gear—repairing what could be salvaged, replacing what couldn't, and trying to remember how rucksacks work without accidentally assembling a hang glider.

Naturally, when we told people we were planning to walk the West Highland Way, the responses ranged from mild amusement to outright horror. "You're *walking* it?" they'd say, as if we'd announced plans to canoe the M25. "Voluntarily?"

Many told us we were mad. Some even looked worried. But we just nodded politely, smiled in that special way reserved for lunatics and cult members, and quietly judged them for choosing to live their entire existence within four walls, surrounded by radiators and scented candles, never knowing the joy of a blister the size of a plum.

They thought *we* were crazy? We thought *they* were insane for never leaving their postcode.

In a rare moment of sensible planning, I bought the *Trailblazer* guide to the West Highland Way and read it cover to cover like it was the last readable thing on Earth. I studied the maps, scribbled notes, and felt the creeping sense that I might, just *might*, actually be prepared.

I also watched YouTube videos made by people who'd already done the walk. Or at least, claimed to. Some of them were useful. Some. The rest were... let's just say I've seen more coherent storytelling from toddlers hopped up on Haribo. I mean, I don't want to sound judgemental—but if you've managed to walk the entire trail and still produced a video that looks like it was filmed on a toaster, edited by a squirrel, and narrated by someone actively bored of their own voice, then you probably shouldn't have bothered.

Some clips were so bad they made me nostalgic for buffering. Honestly, I've seen better content from five-year-olds on TikTok. And they usually involve glitter, a dog, and a suspicious amount of Nutella.

Still, between the good book and the appalling videos, I managed to piece together a rough idea of what we were getting into. I learned where the shops were. What the weather might do (answer: whatever it wants). And most importantly, I learned about Scotland's greatest predator. No, not the deep-fried Mars Bar. The midge.

Ah yes. The Scottish midge. Known far and wide as The National Bird of Scotland, presumably because once you've been pecked to death by a cloud of the little sods, the term feels entirely accurate.

Now, the Scottish Midge—or the *Highland Midge*, to give it its full, terrifying title—is not your average annoying insect. Oh no. This one's cunning. It's coordinated. It hunts in packs. And it has absolutely no respect for your personal space, life goals, or skincare routine.

To counter this airborne menace, I equipped each of us with one of those head nets—yes, the full beekeeper chic—so not only would we not get eaten alive, but we'd also look *absolutely fabulous* doing it. Nothing says "rugged outdoorsman" like wandering through the Highlands looking like you're about to wrestle a swarm of bees for charity.

Interestingly, it's the female midges that bite. Because of course it is. Especially the pregnant ones, who apparently require a blood meal before laying their eggs. The males? They don't bite. They're probably at home, feet up, watching *The Crown* and pretending to help out while mum's off hunting joggers.

I took my preparations seriously. I even looked up the dictionary definition of a midge. It's listed as "a small flying insect that bites humans and animals, especially in wet places." The secondary definition? "A tiny person." Now, while the image of flinging tiny people at Velcro walls or using them as bowling pins *did* cross my mind, I absolutely refuse to make that joke. It's inappropriate. Hilarious, but inappropriate. And sadly, probably frowned upon by the authorities.

So then. How *does* one survive the Scottish midge apocalypse?

Well, there are a few proven methods. The most effective one? Pack up your gear, say goodbye to your dreams, and move 200 miles south. Oxfordshire. Kent. Or just about anywhere that doesn't require a net over your face and a constant state of existential dread. But if, like us, you're stubborn, foolish, or just too far gone, then you're going to need a plan.

Step one: know your enemy. Midges find you by detecting the carbon dioxide you breathe out. So, technically, if you just stop breathing for a bit, they'll leave you alone. Of course, this has the small downside of also *killing you*, so perhaps not ideal for a multi-day hike.

Alternatively, you could time your walk for May. That's before the main midge season kicks off in June. But thanks to global warming—and because nature is a sadist—that season seems to be stretching like a dodgy yoga class. So basically, you've got a brief window between "too cold to enjoy" and "too itchy to survive."

And yes, the west of Scotland is where the midges are worst. You'd think someone would have noticed this when naming the *West* Highland Way. But no. Apparently "Path of Itchy Doom" didn't test well in focus groups.

Now, when—*not if*, mind you—when they bite you, it's properly grim. Their teeth aren't little prickers like a polite mosquito. Oh no. They've got mandibles. Tiny saws. They *saw* their way into your skin like they're trying to win a woodwork competition. Then, to add insult to injury, they spit into the wound. That's right. Spit. Midges are basically tiny flying drunks who slash you open and then gob in the hole.

The saliva stops your blood from clotting, which is thoughtful of them, really. It gives them time to settle in, unpack their bags, and enjoy a leisurely four-minute blood buffet. Charming. At this point, your body steps in and says, "Absolutely not," by releasing histamine to deal with the invasion. Which, of course, is what causes all the itching and swelling.

But don't worry—if you're swelling up like a balloon animal, that just means your immune system is working *really well*. Lucky you! You're basically a superhero. With hives.

Now, since we weren't about to abandon the entire trip and relocate to a midge-free utopia, we had to rely on some *practical* measures. I'd already mentioned the fetching net hat—nothing says "seasoned trekker" like looking like you've lost a fight with a mosquito tent—but there were more tricks up our sweat-drenched sleeves.

Tip number one: keep moving. Midges aren't keen on air movement, which is a shame because neither am I, especially uphill. But if you stop for more than ten seconds, they swarm like they've just heard the dinner bell. So unless you fancy being eaten alive while tying your boots, keep plodding.

Tip number two: stay in the sun. I realise this is Scotland and "sun" is often just a rumour, but if it does make a rare appearance, bask in it like a confused iguana. Midges prefer shade, which makes them the goths of the insect world.

Tip number three: avoid being outside at dawn and dusk. This is when they're at their most active and annoying—basically the insect equivalent of teenagers.

And then, the tip to end all tips. The holy grail of midge defence. Are you ready for this? **Avon Skin So Soft.** I'm not joking. This stuff wasn't designed to repel insects. It was meant to moisturise your skin and make you smell faintly like a florist's handbag. But somewhere along the way, someone noticed that midges *hate it*. Possibly because it reminds them of their ex.

Apparently, it works so well that you can buy it in pubs along the West Highland Way. Imagine that—ordering a pint and a bottle of midgie repellent. "Yes, I'll have a lager, a packet of crisps, and something to stop my face being eaten. Cheers."

It may not stop the rain. It won't fix your blisters. But by the end of the walk, you'll be soft, slightly fragrant, and—if it works—*still in possession of most of your blood*. Result.

Now, to be fair to the midges—and I can't believe I'm saying this—they probably won't do you any *real* harm. A few itchy bites, a bit of rage, some flailing about like you're trying to swat invisible demons. Nothing serious. And if you're one of those lucky sods who midges leave alone, congratulations. You might be producing high levels of a chemical called **ketone**, which apparently acts like a natural repellent. So basically, your weird body odour is doing you a favour. Embrace it.

But just when you think it's safe to go back in the heather... along come the **ticks**.

Ticks don't swarm, they don't buzz, and they don't politely warn you they're about to gnaw into your flesh. They just leap out of a bush, latch on like tiny vampires, and start drinking you dry. Unlike the midges, these things *can* do actual damage—*proper* damage—in the form of Lyme disease.

And let me tell you, Lyme disease is no joke. The first sign is usually a red circular rash around the bite site. But here's the kicker: it can take *months* to show up. And some people don't get the rash at all—they just start feeling like death warmed up, with flu-like symptoms and a vague sense that something's not right, which could describe most of us *at the best of times*, to be fair.

There are horror stories about people suffering for *years* because they didn't catch it early. And since ticks don't wear little signs saying "Hello, I'm infected," the only real defence is being paranoid and checking yourself like you're trying to win a game of biological Where's Wally.

Now, if the midges don't eat you, and the ticks don't inject you with misery, fear not—Scotland still has *plenty* of other creatures that might fancy a nibble. According to official statistics—and I genuinely can't believe someone gets paid to keep track of this—there are an average of **ten animal attacks per day** in Scotland. Mostly dogs. Mostly in Glasgow. Which, frankly, explains itself.

But it's not just dogs. No no. Cows, those gentle-looking grass-munchers, have been known to injure and even *kill* people. Usually dog walkers. Presumably because the cows are sick of Labradors peeing on their ankles.

And then we get into the truly unhinged stuff. In the past decade, there's been a worrying spike in attacks by **rats**, **squirrels**, and **seagulls**. That's right—your average day in the Highlands could end with you being mugged by a rodent or dive-bombed for your chips by something with feathers and zero shame.

And just when you think it can't get weirder... there's been **at least one recorded attack by an alligator. Or a crocodile.** Honestly, I can't remember which—possibly both. Either way, it's the sort of sentence you expect to hear in Florida, not Fife.

To date, no confirmed attacks by Nessie or the wild haggis, although let's be honest—that's probably because **Nessie doesn't leave survivors**, and the haggis is still considered a cryptid by everyone except Scottish uncles after three pints.

Even more bafflingly, these crocodile/alligator attacks *aren't isolated*. In 2019 alone, there were **seven** attacks across the UK. Seven! How has this not made headline news? I'd have expected at least a "...and finally" segment on the BBC: "In other news, a man lost a toe on the fifteenth hole of his local golf course today after being ambushed by a prehistoric death lizard."

But all is not lost. If, by some miracle, you find yourself being chased by a crocodile in the Scottish wilderness, the advice is simple: **run in a zigzag pattern**. Apparently, they're rubbish at corners. That tip came from someone called Dr Sarah Holmes, who sounds like she knows what she's on about, so I'm taking her word for it.

Also, I only have to outrun Robin or Chris. And I like my odds.

Milngavie To Drymen

I'm looking forward to summer, the rain is warmer.

Someone

The long journey north began with suspiciously good omens. The traffic was light, the sky was blue, and fluffy clouds drifted lazily overhead like a Pixar storyboard. Chris was in the back of the car, auditioning for a role as an industrial-strength foghorn, while Robin and I took turns at the wheel, pretending not to notice the slow but steady encroachment of doom.

It was somewhere near Scotch Corner—a place that sounds like it should offer whisky but mainly offers existential despair—when we noticed the sky had stopped being blue and had transitioned into a more threatening shade of "impending sogginess." This wasn't entirely unexpected. We'd checked the weather forecast roughly seven hundred times before setting off and were well aware that our first day of walking would involve heading straight into the path of what meteorologists lovingly call "an absolute soaking."

Now, when I say it was our first day of walking, I use the term "day" in the loosest possible sense. Technically, it would be more of a light saunter squeezed into the back end of the afternoon. By the time we made it to Milngavie, found somewhere to park the car, and shoved something vaguely edible into our faces, we figured we'd get a good few miles under our belts—mainly to reduce the pain of Day Two, but we'll get to that mess later.

As we motored further north, the clouds became moodier than a teenager forced to go on a family camping holiday. We knew precisely when we crossed the invisible border into Scotland because that's when we had to flick on the windscreen wipers. Subtle, yes, but also incredibly damp. With every mile, the drizzle evolved—first into rain, then heavier rain, then into something that felt less like weather and more like personal vengeance from the gods of the Highlands.

By the time we reached Glasgow, we'd stopped checking the forecast because the forecast had clearly given up. We glided into the Clyde Tunnel, that noble feat of engineering designed to funnel drivers directly under a river, and emerged on the other side into what I can only describe as horizontal rain with a grudge. For a solid minute, all three of us just sat there in silence, watching the weather try to unmake the car one droplet at a time, before breaking into hysterical laughter. Because if you don't laugh, you start Googling "holiday refunds."

I wasn't especially worried at this point. We had wet-weather gear so advanced it could probably survive a light bath on the moon. Our plan was simple: get our heads down and march through the deluge like heroic idiots. Besides, the forecast insisted that Monday would be the only washout. The rest of the week, we were promised, would be a more civilised mix of "light showers" and "character-building dampness."

Eventually, we inched through the traffic and rolled into Milngavie, the unpronounceable launchpad of the West Highland Way. Soon enough, we pulled into the car park of the Premier Inn, where we hoped to stash the car for the week. I'd read—somewhere between a blog and a desperate forum post—that the hotel used to let walkers park there in exchange for a donation to their chosen charity: Great Ormond Street Hospital. Of course, that was back in the hazy, pre-pandemic golden age when people shared things like car parks and handshakes. Whether this arrangement still existed in the age of QR codes and mild social distrust remained to be seen—but we were about to find out the fun way.

While Rob and Chris waited in the car, probably arguing about crisps or snoring, I ventured into the reception, almost forgetting my face mask in the way one forgets their trousers—essential, yet inexplicably elusive. I'd plastered on my most charming smile, not that anyone could tell because it was, of course, hidden behind a slab of blue polyester and the creeping awkwardness of post-pandemic small talk.

The receptionist, thankfully, was the kind of person you want to find behind a desk after a five-hour drive through increasingly angry weather —warm, friendly, and not at all fazed by the bedraggled man now sweating into her carpet. She confirmed that yes, we could leave the car there and, if we were so inclined, even leave the keys. Probably wise, considering Robin's tendency to misplace things like keys, wallets, and—once—his entire sense of responsibility.

On one memorable outing along the Yorkshire Wolds Way, we were halfway through the walk when Robin patted his pockets, looked thoughtful, and announced he no longer had his car keys. This was a slight issue, given that we were walking *to* his car, not past it. Our choices were: (a) walk another twelve miles back to *my* car, or (b) scream into a hedge. We opted for both.

Anyway, having confirmed we wouldn't have to sleep in the car like a trio of particularly unprepared hedgehogs, I returned to the vehicle with the gravitas of someone about to deliver bad news. I opened the door, shook my head solemnly and announced that no, we *couldn't* leave the car here after all—and that we'd probably get clamped, fined, or catapulted off the premises. Robin's face crumpled like a wet tissue. I let the tension stew for a second before cracking up. The game was afoot, and so was the mischief.

We moved the car to a more inconspicuous spot at the back of the car park, which, judging by the staff's tone, was probably considered safe because the vehicle looked so utterly battered that no self-respecting thief would touch it. Then came the sacred ritual of Getting Ready. Boots on. Coats zipped. Cagoules deployed. And, in my case, the Hat.

Ah yes, *the Hat*. A wide-brimmed number I wear on most walks. It's functional, dependable, and apparently hilarious. My wife takes particular delight in mocking me for it—usually with phrases like "Indiana Dork" or "Crocodile Dunce"—but I remain unfazed. The hat does what it's supposed to. It blocks the sun when there *is* sun, and it keeps my glasses dry when there definitely isn't. For those lucky enough not to rely on corrective lenses, let me explain: having your specs misted up by sideways rain is the fastest way to feel like a blind mole in a carwash.

Plus, the hat has the added bonus of entertaining everyone else. I've accepted that, fashion-wise, I resemble a man who's lost a bet in a camping shop—but at least I'm a *dry* man who's lost a bet.

I drew the line at the poncho, though. That

monstrous sheet of nylon flaps around like a windswept marquee and is only to be worn in meteorological emergencies. Today's rain, while persistent, wasn't yet biblical. So the poncho remained folded in my pack, sulking.

Next, I gave my boots a final spray with waterproofing wax like a parent sending their child off to school—"Be brave. Be strong. Don't let the puddles win." I've had blisters before. I've had blisters so large they should've been assigned their own postcode. And more than once, I've blamed wet boots. These ones were relatively new—broken in during a charming little weather apocalypse on the Cleveland Way in late 2020—and I was keen not to repeat the Mistakes of Walks Past.

Finally, I hoisted on my rucksack, fashionably lagging behind the others, who were already fully kitted up and giving me the kind of look normally reserved for people who hold up supermarket queues with coupons. The pack had been lovingly adjusted to within an inch of its life for the perfect fit, but actually *getting* it on nearly toppled me backwards like an upended tortoise. It wasn't outrageously heavy—around twenty kilos—but it had enough mass to warp time slightly if I moved too fast.

Somehow, I stayed upright, to the visible disappointment of Rob and Chris, who were clearly hoping for a comedy fall to start the day. No such luck. I staggered into position, we locked the car, and then made our way back to reception.

There, we dropped off the keys and made a suitably generous donation to the charity box—as thanks for the parking and possibly for emotional support in advance. We waved goodbye to the receptionist, promised we'd be back in a week (hopefully not as puddles), and officially began our walk.

Milngavie—pronounced, for reasons known only to ancient druids and possibly some drunk linguists, as "Mull-guy"—is a small town that manages to bewilder both the eyes and the ears. I consider myself reasonably well-versed in Britain's rich tapestry of place-name nonsense (hello again, Mousehole and Alnwick), but Milngavie took the crown. It sounds like the name of someone's elderly aunt, not a launchpad for a 96-mile hike through the Highlands.

As we trudged north along a moderately busy road, trying not to get clipped by enthusiastic locals in hatchbacks, we were greeted with smiles, nods, and the occasional "good luck" shouted across the drizzle. Spirits were high. Morale was solid. Our confidence levels hovered somewhere near delusional. In our heads, this was a done deal. Success rate? A smug and unshakeable one hundred per cent.

Soon enough, we stumbled into the centre of

town and located the official starting point of the West Highland Way: a rather dignified obelisk on Douglas Street, standing proudly like a granite exclamation mark saying, "You lot are going to regret this." Handily, right next to this symbol of grandeur and impending blisters was a coffee shop. And given that we'd endured a staggering thirty-metre march from the car park, we decided we'd earned a reward.

In we went, like drowned cats seeking both caffeine and central heating. Hot chocolates were ordered with all the desperation of Victorian orphans, and we immediately began shedding layers of rainwear like molting reptiles. There we were, tucked away in the far corner, steaming quietly in our own microclimate, creating puddles on the floor and looking like the sort of customers a café owner sees in a fever dream.

We were, unsurprisingly, the subject of some amused interest. A table of pensioners, clearly enjoying their outing and their dry clothes, gave us the kind of looks reserved for people trying to eat soup with forks. One of them—resplendent in a majestic blue rinse—leaned over and offered hearty congratulations, clearly assuming we had just *finished* the West Highland Way, not just *started* it.

Chris, bless him, politely corrected her and explained that no, we were just setting off, and that he merely looked like death because he was slightly hungover, not broken by the Highlands. There was a pause. Then laughter. Real, genuine, belly-shaking pensioner laughter. They returned to their tea and tittered into their teacakes. Our earlier 100% success rating quietly revised itself to "optimistically 87%."

Meanwhile, I was wrestling with my phone in a futile attempt to scan the table's track-and-trace QR code. This, in the twilight days of pandemic protocol, was the ticket to being allowed to sit anywhere without feeling like a health risk. Unfortunately, my phone flatly refused to acknowledge that the code existed. Chris and Rob tried too, with equally useless results. After several increasingly undignified attempts involving angling the phone, adjusting the brightness, and squinting like confused meerkats, we admitted defeat.

Rob scribbled his details on a slip of paper and handed it to the staff like a schoolboy turning in late homework. We speculated that our failure may have had something to do with trying to use the *English* app in *Scotland*, as if the virus itself respected borders. We never did get a proper answer, but by then the hot chocolate had kicked in, our coats were dripping more slowly, and we had places to be. Wet, slippery places.

Although it was finally time to bid farewell to Milngavie and get this long trudge north underway, it felt rude—ungrateful, even—to just march off without acknowledging the town's greatest contribution to human civilisation: the frankly unhinged genius of one George Bennie. Now, I realise I have a tendency to veer off on historical tangents like a dog chasing a squirrel, but trust me, this one is absolutely worth the detour.

George Bennie is not a household name. He's not even a shed name. In fact, unless you're either an engineering enthusiast or the sort of person who collects train numbers for fun and definitely not for therapy, chances are you've never heard of him. I certainly hadn't. But that changes today, because George Bennie deserves your attention.

Now, before anyone gets offended, let me just say: nerds are brilliant. Nerds run the world. Without nerds, we wouldn't have things like Wi-Fi, cashpoints, or unnecessarily complicated coffee machines. Steve Jobs started his empire in a garage, which is as nerdy as it gets. If one of my kids ever started doing that, I'd be equal parts proud and suspicious, mostly because we don't *have* a garage, and I'd want to know where the hell it came from.

Anyway—back to Bennie. George Bennie was a Scottish genius, although you wouldn't know it because he's spent most of history being overshadowed by the flashier kids at the genius table—namely Alexander Graham Bell and John Logie Baird. Bell gave us the telephone, Baird gave us the television, and between them they've laid the groundwork for most of modern civilisation's decline into overstimulation, selfie culture, and Love Island.

Not that I'm bitter. I love a bit of telly, and my phone has essentially grafted itself to my hand at this point, but when you regularly see people walking down the street *watching television* on their *phones* while simultaneously stepping into traffic, you do begin to wonder if maybe, just *maybe*, we took a wrong turn somewhere in the 1980s. Still, at least they occasionally walk into lamp posts, which is hilarious and counts as natural justice in my book.

Now, while Bell and Baird got all the glory (and the posh medals), there's also James Goodfellow, another proud Scot, and inventor of the cash machine. Thanks to him, we can now go overdrawn faster and with more style than ever before—especially after five pints and a poorly thought-out craving for flaming sambuca and an industrial-grade kebab. Based on my own detailed research, this is also the reason your card gets declined three days later while attempting to buy teabags in Tesco, causing you shame, panic, and a stern tut from the retired colonel behind you who clearly thinks you should've brought exact change and a sense of decorum.

But George Bennie didn't mess around with phone calls or money machines. No, no. He gave the world something infinitely more glorious: *the Railplane*. Yes, the Railplane—because what the world really needed in the 1930s was a vehicle that looked like a train, sounded like a plane, and promised the practicality of neither.

The Bennie Railplane was, and I'm being entirely serious here, a high-speed, propeller-powered train suspended from an overhead rail. Think Jules Verne, with a splash of steampunk and a pinch of "maybe don't operate heavy machinery while drinking." Propellers at both ends meant the train could zoom forwards, stop on a dime, or reverse dramatically—possibly while sounding like a blender full of wasps. Bennie, being the eco-conscious visionary he was, also made provisions for multiple power sources: diesel, electricity, and —brace yourself—recycled cow farts. Truly, the man was ahead of his time and possibly out of his mind.

The whole thing hung from a sleek metal rail supported by towering pylons, so it could soar above existing railways, roads, and small woodland creatures without getting in anyone's way. It was pitched as the perfect futuristic solution: it didn't require new routes, avoided level crossings, and didn't force the government to build 500 new bridges every time someone wanted to cross a stream.

Now, granted, one might question the logic of building an entirely separate train system directly *above* the existing one. If your big selling point is "It won't interfere with old trains because it's flying above them," then you do have to wonder whether the old trains needed replacing in the first place. But this was 1930, and enthusiasm regularly outpaced practicality.

Amazingly, Bennie managed to raise the funds to build a full-sized, working prototype right here in Milngavie. It opened with great fanfare on Tuesday, 8th July 1930 (because apparently Tuesday is the optimum day for revolutionising public transport), and the launch was attended by a gaggle of dignitaries, engineers, and newspaper men—all in suits and hats so dapper they made Downton Abbey look like a stag do in Benidorm.

Sadly, despite all the pomp and propellers, the Railplane never quite, well... took off. Pun absolutely intended. It trundled into the history books with more rust than glory, sat decaying on its track for years, and was finally scrapped in 1956. Bennie died a year later, presumably heartbroken, and his dream went with him—relegated to the great scrapyard of forgotten genius.

Which is a shame, because frankly, I'd *love* to live in a world where sleek little railplanes whizz above the countryside, run on eco-puffs and nostalgia, and occasionally offer you a complimentary mint. Compared to some of the stuff we've had to endure on British trains lately—delays, cancellations, and toilets that smell like despair—I think Bennie was onto something.

Admittedly, there's the tiny issue of propeller blades spinning furiously at head height near platforms, turning careless commuters into fine mincemeat. But apart from that minor bloodbath, I can't see any real downside. In fact, I can think of a few former fellow passengers I wouldn't mind accidentally nudging in the direction of a high-speed propeller. But perhaps that's just me.

Bennie's carriages, by the way, were delightful little contradictions. Streamlined exteriors, automatic sliding doors (decades before they were a thing), and the sort of wood-panelled, curtained interiors that screamed Victorian comfort reimagined by someone who once saw the future in a dream. There were plush individual chairs, reading lamps, and tables that didn't wobble like jelly in an earthquake. British Rail, take notes.

But—and here's the final gut punch—Bennie's invention wasn't even the first of its kind. The Germans, naturally, got there first. In 1901, they launched the Schwebebahn in Wuppertal: a suspended train that ran gracefully above the River Wupper. I discovered this marvel back in 1989 during an exchange trip, staying with my penfriend Dirk near Cologne. Dirk's dad took us on a day trip and gleefully shared the amazing tale of the local hanging train, which somehow managed to be both brilliant and terrifying. Like rollercoasters. Or Aldi wine.

And just when I thought the Schwebebahn couldn't get any more bonkers, Dirk's dad dropped a bombshell of a story that's stuck with me ever since. Brace yourself. On the 21st of July, 1950, an elephant fell to its death into the river below. Yes, you read that correctly. An elephant fell off a train. This was apparently part of an attempt to demonstrate how strong the train was, which—as sales pitches go—feels wildly optimistic. But even that isn't quite the whole story.

To understand this majestic debacle, we must rewind to the arrival of the Althoff Circus in the fine German town of Wuppertal. Now, Franz Althoff, the circus trainer and PR stunt enthusiast, had a bit of a tradition: wherever the circus went, he'd parade Tuffi the elephant through town on the local tram. You know, as you do.

Unfortunately, Wuppertal didn't *have* trams. What it *did* have was the Schwebebahn—an upside-down monorail that dangles above the River Wupper like something out of a steampunk fever dream. So naturally, Althoff looked at this precarious, sky-suspended contraption and thought: "Yes. Let's put the elephant *on that*."

Shockingly, this did not go entirely to plan.

Unlike the friendly, flat trams of yesteryear, the Schwebebahn had the unnerving habit of tilting dramatically around corners. Tuffi, being unaccustomed to hanging two stories above a river in a swaying metal sausage, became alarmed. She trumpeted in confusion, panicked, and then —presumably fuelled by equal parts terror and disbelief—charged through the side of the carriage and flung herself into the river below. Presumably, she expected to find a nice hallway or some hay on the other side, only to discover gravity instead.

Before we move on, we should take a moment to appreciate the utter chaos of that day, the *21st of July*, which has clearly been appointed by the universe as the official day for absolute carnage.

Some days in history are quiet. Nothing much happens. Like my birthday, for example. But *not* the 21st of July. That's the date history puts on its party trousers and starts flipping tables.

For starters, it's the anniversary of the first major battle of the American Civil War, which —spoiler alert—wasn't terribly civil. It also saw Wild Bill Hickok kill his first man in what's now considered the inaugural proper western showdown. You know the kind: two sweaty men squint at each other, draw pistols, and hope for the best. Jesse James also committed his first train robbery on this date. Completely unrelated, obviously, but it does make you wonder whether something particularly chaotic happens in the cosmos around mid-July.

And there's more. *So* much more.

On the same date, an airship named the *Wingfoot* plummeted through the glass ceiling of the Illinois Trust and Savings Bank in Chicago, which is definitely one of the worst places to unexpectedly arrive uninvited. (And yes, if you read my last book on the Yorkshire Wolds, you'll recall how unreasonably excited I get about airships. No regrets.)

Still not done. On this day, a Frenchman named Louis Rigolly became the first human to drive at 100mph, which kicked off a proud national tradition of driving like absolute lunatics. Want proof? Drive through rural France. Blink and you'll miss the Renault doing 110 past your wing mirror.

But oh no, the Brits couldn't let the French have their moment, could they? Years later—*on the same day*, naturally—Sir Malcolm Campbell smashed the 150mph barrier, presumably just to annoy Rigolly and anyone else in Europe with a stopwatch and a speedometer.

What else? Oh yes. The Americans invaded Guam. The French invaded the Isle of Wight (accidentally, one assumes), and Hitler had a bit of a tantrum and executed the folks who'd tried to assassinate him the day before. Chilly stuff. Speaking of which, on this very same date, the *coldest temperature ever recorded on Earth* happened at Vostok Station in Antarctica: -89.2°C. That's colder than Scotland in February, and we all know that's saying something.

And, as if that wasn't enough cosmic madness for one date, the NASA space shuttle *Atlantis* touched down for the final time, ending the entire shuttle programme—on the *exact same date* Bennie launched his Railplane back in 1930. Coincidence? Maybe. But I'm watching you, 21st of July.

Oh, and again, just to recap: *an elephant fell off a train*.

Now, back to business.

The press, who had been invited aboard to witness this thrilling PR stunt, were presumably caught slightly off guard by the sudden presence of airborne pachyderm. No genuine photos of the incident exist, which is probably for the best. There is *one* image doing the rounds, but it's so obviously fake it might as well feature a flying pig and a unicorn riding in a sidecar. Even the tabloids didn't try to pass it off as real, which is how you *really* know it wasn't.

When I recounted this tale to my wife, she wasn't impressed. She launched into a passionate speech about animal rights and why this sort of thing absolutely *wasn't funny*. I got told off, properly. But I stand by it. If *you* fell through the side of a moving train into a river, I'd laugh. Not for long, obviously—I'd make sure you were okay first—but I *would* laugh. Equality demands I do the same for elephants. It's only fair.

Anyway, fear not—Tuffi didn't die. Quite the opposite, in fact. She suffered only minor injuries and, like anyone who's ever tripped on a pavement while trying to look cool, was probably far more embarrassed than hurt. You know the drill: you fall, then immediately look around to see who witnessed your shame. Everyone did. Everyone *always* does. But you pretend otherwise and walk on, trying to reclaim some shred of dignity.

Tuffi, bless her, carried on with circus life for a while before moving to France to work for another circus, which must have been a bit of a culture shock. I mean, how many elephants speak fluent French? Still, she made it through and eventually passed away peacefully in 1989, presumably nowhere near any railways or bridges, which is a nice thought. Though it does leave one final, lingering question:

What *do* you do with four tonnes of dead elephant?

Answers on a postcard.

I'm snapped back into the present by the cold slap of reality: it is, unfortunately, *actually* time to leave. As much as I'd have happily stayed in that café until the weather improved, or society collapsed—whichever came first—it was time to get moving. One foot in front of the other. Repeat until either Fort William or death.

With no one able to come up with a legitimate

excuse to stay indoors ("the floor is flat" didn't quite cut it), we reluctantly wriggled back into our wet-weather gear, hoisted on our rucksacks, thanked the staff for tolerating our dripping, mildly pungent presence, and headed back outside —taking out a pensioner or two with our oversized backpacks in the process. I did cheekily invite one of the blue-rinse brigade to join us on the walk, but she politely declined with a grin and the magnificent line: "I did it years ago. I'm not that stupid anymore." Fair play.

Of course, no great expedition can begin without an obligatory photo at the starting obelisk. We dutifully posed, took turns photographing each other for posterity, and then made a valiant yet doomed attempt at a group selfie—three heads, two arms, one phone, and the creeping awkwardness of a damp, preposterously bundled-up trio trying to look heroic while avoiding misting up the lens.

Thanks to the pandemic, the age-old tradition of "Excuse me, would you mind taking a quick photo of us?" had become a game of social Russian roulette. Some people would happily snap a dozen pictures and ask about your route, others would react as though you'd just licked their child. I was firmly in the "I'll take your photo, it's not like I'm going to catch anything off your phone" camp. But society, it seemed, wasn't always in agreement.

Photos acquired, off we trotted. We passed

beneath a large, hopeful-looking sign declaring the name of the trail, then ambled past a series of chunky metal sculptures—each one representing a location along the West Highland Way. Chris, with camera in hand, photographed every single one like a man possessed. At his pace, we'd be lucky to reach Fort William by September.

Soon the path opened into a gentle riverside stroll—idyllic, if you ignored the drizzle and the fact your socks were now 40% lake. Then, without warning, the trail got hilly. Not mountains, exactly, but enough undulation to remind your calves they were about to become very well acquainted with pain. Dog walkers and couples littered the path, all chirping "hello" or "good luck" as they passed, which was nice. Polite, friendly, and just the right amount of smug from those who were clearly only doing a 20-minute loop and would be back home in the bath with a cuppa by the time we hit mile three.

A mile or so in—at the top of yet another deceptive incline—we stopped to chat with a pair of women who'd walked the route a few years back. They were full of stories. Glorious weather, charming hotels, lively pubs overflowing with music, laughter, and industrial quantities of beer. One of them explained she wouldn't walk it again, not because it had been bad, but because it had been *perfect*, and she didn't want to mess with the memory—especially not on a day like this, she added, casting a pitying glance at our damp faces. A confidence booster, that.

But I got it. We'd done the Coast to Coast back in 2016, and it had been the walking equivalent of winning the lottery and getting a foot massage at the same time. Perfect weather, great company, barely a blister between us. We'd talked about doing it again, but deep down, we all knew it wouldn't be the same. And now it never could be. One of our group, Graham, had since passed away. Without him, the idea of going back felt hollow. Some things are best left as golden memories.

Rain continued to patter down as we said our goodbyes and carried on north, weaving through more trees and up and down hills that weren't exactly Everest, but which still managed to be thoroughly annoying. That said, the exertion was at least warming us up. Layers that had once been soaked and freezing were now just soaked and slightly steamy.

By this point, we were skirting the southern edge of Mugdock Country Park, which, surprisingly, was still teeming with walkers—most of them armed with dogs and the grim determination of people who go out *regardless*. Many were probably headed to Mugdock Castle, plonked in the middle of the park and recently given a little showbiz makeover.

You see, the castle featured in the 2018 film

Outlaw King, starring Chris Pine as Robert the Bruce. It's a historical epic with just enough truth to keep the historians grumbling and just enough artistic licence to keep the actors looking good. When filming, the crew went full medieval and built an entire period village on-site, just to make it feel authentic. And fair play to them—they did a bang-up job. The whole thing looked incredible, even if the script took a few liberties. But then again, if Hollywood can make Russell Crowe Scottish and Kevin Costner English, anything's possible.

Rounding Scroggy Hill—an excellent name for a hill, by the way, sounding like either a minor Dickensian villain or an especially grumpy dwarf —the path finally straightened out after all the meandering nonsense. Just ahead lay Craigallian Loch, its surface shimmering in the drizzle like a soggy postcard from the Campsie Fells to the north-east.

Rob and Chris were, as usual, a few yards ahead of me. This had become the standard formation over the years: they lead, I follow. Their natural walking pace was only a fraction faster than mine—barely noticeable over the course of a hundred yards, but after a mile or two they were comfortably out of conversational range, which suited everyone just fine.

I didn't mind trailing behind. It gave me a chance to enjoy the peace, soak up the scenery, and occasionally pretend I was Bear Grylls minus the urine-drinking. And it didn't bother them either, since it meant they got to pause every now and then, rest their legs, and hurl insults at me like the supportive friends they are. Besides, I'd catch them on the hills. Rob, bless him, has many qualities, but speed on an incline isn't one of them. Chris once called him a "big unit," which is quite possibly the politest way to describe someone built like a rugby forward in a fleece.

Chris, by contrast, is the anti-Rob. Short by modern standards, but absurdly agile. He approaches hills like a mountain goat on espresso —springing ahead of us with terrifying efficiency and always waiting at the top with a smug grin and an open bag of Haribo, like some kind of sugary summit troll.

As I trudged along behind them, I passed the Craigallian Fire Memorial, and I wondered if the other two had even noticed it—what with their heads down, eyes squinting through rain, and minds probably occupied with Haribo logistics. Which would be a shame, because the Craigallian Fire is no ordinary rock with a plaque. It marks a moment, a movement, and an absolutely flaming miracle.

The stone's inscription reads:

Here burned the Craigallian Fire. During the Depression of the 1930s, it was a beacon of

companionship and hope for young unemployed people who came from Glasgow and Clydebank seeking adventure in Scotland's wild places. Their pioneering spirit helped to make the Scottish countryside free for all to roam.

Now just pause a second and take that in. This wasn't some symbolic fire mentioned in a poem— this thing actually burned *non-stop* from the early 1920s right up to the start of the Second World War. And even then, it only dimmed slightly, reportedly still burning during the day. That's not just a fire—that's a full-blown metaphor with kindling.

But it wasn't just about warmth and tea. This was a meeting place. A rallying point. During those hard years—post-World War One, pre-any-hope-of-a-decent-job—the fire drew Glasgow's unemployed youth into the wilds. They walked, they talked, they brewed questionable tea in rusty kettles, and they discussed politics, rights, and the slightly controversial notion that just maybe they should be allowed to walk on hills without being shot at by a landowner with an inferiority complex.

It wasn't the only fire burning around here, but it's the one that entered legend. Big names passed through: Tom Weir, the red-hatted climbing icon of Scotland, and Hamish Brown, who invented the frankly exhausting concept of Munro bagging —climbing all 282 of Scotland's mountains over

3,000 feet. That's fine if you've got strong knees, no job, and a death wish, but otherwise, maybe just admire them from a nice café.

The fireside chats of those trailblazers lit the way—literally and figuratively—for what would eventually become Scotland's first National Park: Loch Lomond and the Trossachs. You'd think such a stunning, iconic place would have been declared a National Park in the 19th century, or at least sometime between the invention of jam and the iPod. But no. It didn't officially open its metaphorical gates until the *24th of April, 2002*. Yes, that's right—*2002*. About five minutes ago in historical terms.

Even more scandalous? Scotland has just *two* National Parks. Two. In a country that looks like it was designed by Tolkien and blessed by David Attenborough, that is borderline criminal. And here's the kicker: the first ever National Park *anywhere* in the world was Yellowstone in the USA, established in 1890. And who was instrumental in getting it protected? A Scot. John flaming Muir. Born in Dunbar, and clearly not a fan of sheep, which he referred to as "hoofed locusts." Harsh, but relatable.

I couldn't tell Rob or Chris any of what I'd just read on the Craigallian Fire memorial because, by the time I looked up, they'd already marched ahead like two lads late for a sale at Go Outdoors. Eventually, though, they stopped near a small wooden shack, and I caught up, soaked but spiritually buoyant. We stood for a moment admiring a cluster of huts nearby—though to call them *huts* felt slightly misleading. They were more like small, rustic houses that had politely declined to become bungalows.

The rain hadn't let up, of course—why would it? —and I found myself eyeing one of the huts with thinly veiled envy. One in particular was built on stilts, as though anticipating a biblical flood or perhaps just a very angry badger. I turned to Rob and Chris and suggested, only half-joking, that we sleep under it for the night. At that point, the idea of crawling under some wooden stilts and lying in the mud like a raccoon with a mortgage seemed almost appealing.

And yet, even in that dripping moment of damp despair, I smiled to myself. That old cliché—*I'd rather be hiking in the rain than stuck at a desk on a sunny day*—came to mind, and, annoyingly, it still held true. Even now. Even in this sideways rain. Even with wet underwear.

Tucked somewhere in the trees to our left were more huts, hidden from the path, forming part of the legendary little community of *Carbeth*. And if you've never heard of it, don't worry—you're probably not a hutting enthusiast. Yes, "hutting." It's a real thing. It means exactly what it sounds like: people who are deeply passionate about living in huts in the woods. Not glamping, not Airbnb, not rustic-chic cottages with underfloor heating—*actual huts*.

Carbeth began after the First World War, when returning soldiers needed somewhere to convalesce that wasn't full of noise, smog, or people asking them if they were "feeling better yet." Later, during the economic meltdown that followed, the community grew as people from Clydebank and the rougher corners of Glasgow scraped together pennies to rent these humble shelters, drawn by the promise of fresh, clean air.

Then came the Second World War, and with it the Blitz. Entire families fled the city and moved out here to live in the woods full-time. Not quite Centre Parcs, but it did the job. Post-war, the eco-brigade moved in—people seeking the simple life, the quiet life, the no-running-water-and-definitely-no-internet life. Carbeth became a tiny utopia. But as with all utopias, someone eventually tried to ruin it.

Towards the end of the 20th century, the local landowner did what local landowners do best: decided he wanted more money. Rents were hiked up, presumably in the hope of pricing everyone out so he could build a golf course, a shooting lodge, or whatever it is that landlords dream of while stroking their spaniels and sipping sherry.

But the hutters didn't fold. They banded together, formed a collective, and basically went full Robin Hood. There were bitter confrontations, tales of intimidation, and even people being *burned out of their huts*—which, to be clear, is not a metaphor. Yet somehow, they pulled together, raised the funds, and bought the land outright, securing the future of Carbeth and ensuring that no one could evict them again—not even the sherry-drinking spaniel man.

They still have no mains water, no electricity, and no convenient Amazon delivery slots. But they've got the trees, the hills, and the smug satisfaction of knowing that no one can tell them to leave. That said, I did spare a thought for them as I stood there dripping. I hoped, for their sake, it didn't always rain like this.

After Carbeth, we joined a small road heading west for about half a mile. Thankfully it was relatively traffic-free, and the few cars that did pass gave us a generous berth, probably assuming we were either local nutters or part of a sponsored walk to raise awareness for waterproof trousers. Not that a tidal wave from a passing hatchback would've made any difference—we were already wetter than a fish's pocket.

Then Robin spotted a sign stapled to a fence advertising something glorious: *Kip in the Kirk*, a hostel in Drymen (which, of course, is pronounced *Drimmen*, because Scottish pronunciation is basically a game of Scrabble with a vendetta). The sign may as well have said "Free pizza and hot baths for drowned hikers."

We had originally planned to camp. You know, in *this*. In what had by now developed into a fully-fledged monsoon with emotional issues. Robin suggested we ditch that idea and aim for the hostel instead. Chris and I agreed before he'd even finished the sentence. The romance of camping under the stars is all well and good until the stars are replaced by lightning and your tent starts taking on water like a lifeboat with a death wish.

Hostel it was.

We soon turned off the road and into what can only be described as a field-shaped puddle. A young family stood nearby, clearly in the early stages of rethinking their life plans for the day. They were debating whether to walk up a hill in clothes better suited to a summer picnic in Surrey. As we sloshed past, they quietly gave up on the whole endeavour and turned back toward their car —and, one assumes, their centrally heated home, complete with dry socks and emotional stability.

As we climbed the hill, I found myself reflecting on how entirely *unsurprising* it is that the inventor of the raincoat, Charles Macintosh, hailed from nearby Glasgow. Honestly, if this was the default weather setting, inventing waterproof clothing was less about innovation and more about sheer survival. If he hadn't done it, someone else would've just wrapped themselves in baked beans tins and called it fashion.

Despite the soggy gloom, the view from the top wasn't bad at all. In fact, it was quite good. I could only imagine how spectacular it might be on a day when the sky wasn't actively wailing on us. And that's when the existential doubts began to creep in. What *were* we doing? We'd been out for hours in steadily worsening weather, trudging through waterlogged landscapes for what, exactly? Walk the West Highland Way, they said. *See the beautiful Scottish countryside*, they said. So far, all we'd seen was a hill through the bottom of a puddle.

And then, in a rare twist of cosmic mercy, the clouds parted. For roughly seven seconds. The sun appeared like a guest arriving halfway through their own party, and even the buzzard circling above us seemed surprised by this break in the biblical gloom.

We rounded Dumgoyach, a lovely squat hill with a name that sounds like something you'd mutter after sneezing. Somewhere up there, apparently, were the ancient Dumgoyach Stones—sacred, mysterious, and very much *not* seen by us. We were genuinely looking for them too, but the weather, the puddles, and possibly the wrath of ancient spirits conspired to keep them hidden.

I'd also hoped to catch a glimpse of Duntreath Castle, which looms somewhere just beyond the hill. It's a delightful little fairytale sort of place—if your fairytales involve private land and a slight air of decline. We missed that too. Probably needed to be halfway up a tree to see it.

Duntreath has been the ancestral home of the Edmonstone family for generations. Most of them, historically speaking, were a bit dull. But the 3rd Baronet, Sir Archibald, stood out for all the wrong reasons. He went off to Egypt, poked around in tombs, wrote a few deeply unreadable books, and —naturally—married his cousin. All while being perpetually sozzled, which probably explains the cousin bit.

His literary contributions include such snoozefests as *The Christian Gentleman's Daily Walk* and *Thoughts on the Observance of Lent*, which I can only assume were written specifically to help people fall asleep before the invention of Ambien. His historical legacy is, let's say, *quiet*. Like, whisper-in-an-empty-library quiet.

Sadly, all the couple's children died in infancy, which is tragic. Though they did at least have a nice castle to mope about in. As for the 4th Baronet, Sir William? He earns his place in trivia quizzes by being the great-great-grandfather of none other than Camilla, Duchess of Cornwall. So there you go—ancestral castles, cousin marriages, and whisky-fuelled Egyptology, all neatly tied to our Queen Consort.

Back on the path, we joined a long, arrow-straight track—clearly an old railway line, based on how suspiciously flat it was. The rain returned with the kind of enthusiasm you usually reserve for party guests who refuse to leave. I recognised the area now. Our original plan had included a stop at the famed *Glengoyne Distillery*, which lay just ahead.

I had been looking forward to that. I'd never visited a distillery before, and there was something deeply appealing about learning how they turned cold rain and despair into liquid joy. Sadly, it wasn't the weather that ruined the plan, but COVID. The place was open—but visits had to be booked in advance. And given we couldn't even guess what *hour* we'd get there, never mind which day, it wasn't to be. A true shame. I had imagined wandering among copper stills, sipping a dram, and declaring things "peaty" or "complex" while secretly just enjoying not being outside.

But alas. As Robert Burns himself once said, *"The best-laid plans of mice and men aft go completely to crap when you don't book a distillery tour in advance."* Or something like that.

I gazed longingly at the distillery as we passed, picturing the warm interiors, the hum of copper machinery, the gentle buzz of a first whisky… and the overwhelming danger of going in. Because let's be honest: if we'd gone inside, we probably wouldn't have come back out. *Ever*.

To the east, behind the distillery, rose Dumgoyne Hill and the Campsie Fells—stunning, cinematic, and surprisingly famous. We'd be passing through several filming locations on our walk, and this was our first proper one.

These hills, believe it or not, stood in for *South Africa* in the 1983 Monty Python film *The Meaning of Life*. Specifically, they feature in the scene where Zulus attack a British camp, and John Cleese, playing a gloriously indifferent officer, fusses not about the massacre but about a mosquito bite on one of his men, Perkins—played by Eric Idle. Said mosquito has allegedly removed half his leg.

Why that scene? Because the cast and crew had spent a few nights filming up here and been absolutely *devoured* by Scottish midges. So, in classic Python fashion, they commemorated the horror with satire. The leg-eating mosquito is less a comment on insects and more a loving tribute to the real, tiny terrors of the Highlands.

And let me tell you, artistic exaggeration or not, the midge absolutely deserves its own horror film. Preferably one in which it gets what's coming to it.

Somewhere ahead, through the drizzle and our steadily declining morale, was the promise of tea. Specifically, a café I'd heard good things about— the *Beech Tree*. It was said to be warm, welcoming, and exactly the sort of place that might rescue three sodden hikers from the brink of trench foot and emotional collapse.

The rain was no longer just falling—it was *permeating.* It had seeped through supposedly waterproof jackets, bypassed carefully waxed boots, and begun infiltrating our very souls. So yes, a cuppa and a brief thawing session were no longer a luxury—they were a medical necessity.

And then, through the mist like a holy beacon, the café emerged. The glow from the windows practically hummed with the promise of warmth, radiators, and maybe even a biscuit. We made our way toward the entrance, robes of rain trailing behind us like drowned monks. The lights within glowed a soft amber. It was everything a weary walker could want.

Then it all went wrong.

As Rob stepped through the doorway, he was brought to an abrupt halt by a young woman standing directly in his path. Chris walked straight into Rob. I walked straight into both of them. We resembled a very wet and poorly choreographed game of human dominoes. Any passer-by might have found the scene hilarious—if we hadn't looked like extras from *The Perfect Storm.*

From within the café came a voice that could curdle oat milk: "Can I *help* you?" Not "Hello!" or "Come in, you poor drenched souls!" Just those four words, in the exact tone used by people who *absolutely* cannot help you and deeply resent having to ask.

Rob, ever the diplomat, explained that we were hoping to come in for a cup of tea and a warm-up, what with being slightly more water than man at this point.

The woman gave us a long, appraising look. Not the sort of look that says "Oh you poor dears," but rather, "I see you, I disapprove, and I'm not afraid to let you know it." She then informed us that she couldn't give us a table *just for tea*, but she could do takeaway drinks. And we could sit outside. In the rain. At a wet table. Like idiots.

We stared at her. Then at each other. Then back at her. This was… unexpected. Every review I'd read about the Beech Tree had raved about the place—how welcoming it was, how friendly the staff were, how you'd leave with a full belly and a warmed heart. Instead, here we were, dripping on the threshold like Victorian street urchins being told the soup kitchen was full.

She elaborated. There were tables *outside*. We could sit at one of those, if we *really* wanted. She didn't actually say "and perish of exposure," but the implication was very much there. She had now physically barred the doorway, arms folded like a nightclub bouncer for the world's saddest rave. Her glare said everything her words didn't: "See that gate? I want you on the other side of it. Now."

So we turned and left, heads hung low, puddles

forming in our boots. Chris and Rob started the backstroke down the path while I opted for the doggy paddle. Somewhere, a tiny violin played just for us.

As we shuffled away, I looked back, fully intending to give her the kind of death stare that could cause mild discomfort—but she already had one of her own. Hers came pre-installed. I found myself wondering who had stolen her joy, her hope, her last biscuit. Who had eaten her bowl of sunshine that morning and left her with this sour husk of customer service?

What made it worse was the sense of betrayal. I *wanted* to like the Beech Tree. I had *read* the signs. Literally. Their quirky chalkboards promising cosy hospitality and warm welcomes. Maybe it was a pandemic policy, maybe it was a staffing issue, or maybe it was just a bad day. But when we needed them most—three miserable hikers in desperate need of a brew—they closed the door on us.

Figuratively *and* literally.

We rejoined the long, straight stretch of disused railway line, which had now fully embraced its new role as an inland waterway. It wasn't so much a footpath as a trench system. We danced and teetered along it like contestants in a very niche episode of *Strictly Come Drenched*, clinging to whatever dry patch we could find—which was, let's be honest, none at all.

Gorse bushes closed in on both sides like nature's barbed wire, occasionally swiping at our faces with the enthusiasm of a caffeinated cat. Progress slowed to a crawl, and it wasn't long before the rain—now confidently torrential—had made it through every so-called waterproof layer I owned. Cold water found its way onto my skin in several unwelcome locations. Still, I told myself, at least my feet were dry. At which exact moment, I stepped directly into a puddle with all the depth and subtlety of a duck pond.

To say we weren't having the best of days would be a wild understatement. At this point, the *best* part of the day had been not being struck by lightning. Yet.

We paused beneath a bridge for a brief moment of shelter, joining forces with another rain-slicked soul who had also taken refuge. She told us, without so much as a trace of irony or visible trauma, that she had *run* from Milngavie to Balmaha earlier and was now *running back*. That's a round trip of about 38 miles, in monsoon conditions, for fun.

Naturally, we concluded she was completely and irreversibly mad.

We had, in the planning phase of this walk (back when we were dry and deluded), toyed with the idea of taking a side trip to the Devil's Pulpit. It was just off to the west of our current location and supposedly very beautiful—blood-red water coursing through sandstone gorges, mystical atmosphere, all that good stuff. Druids, witches, and the devil himself have allegedly been linked to the place. But as we stood shivering beneath a bridge, looking like discarded laundry, we collectively decided that any thoughts of "detouring" had been drowned somewhere around hour two.

So we trudged on northward, dodging puddles with all the grace of hippos in ballet slippers. The old railway line stretched straight ahead like a challenge from the gods, and off to our right, a small wood sat quietly—peaceful, still, and, as I cheerfully informed Rob and Chris, *full of corpses*.

Specifically, eco-friendly corpses. The wood just north of the village of Killearn is a natural burial ground. You get buried in a biodegradable coffin, no headstone, just a tree planted above your remains. Very green. Very poetic. And I imagined the trees did quite well around here, what with that unique combination of human compost and excessive moisture. You could basically reincarnate yourself into a redwood.

I also theorised—entirely unprovoked—that the presence of this woodland cemetery might have something to do with the fact that George Buchanan was born in Killearn. He was a famous humanist and historian, and while I had no concrete evidence to back this up, it felt like the kind of leap a local council might make in a PowerPoint pitch: "Historical figure… humanist… let's plant bodies under trees." That sort of thing.

Eventually, we reached the next road crossing, and with it, another sign for Kip in the Kirk. I took it as a divine reminder that, yes, we *were* still heading for salvation—and that maybe we should phone ahead before a tragic twist of fate robbed us of our dry bunks.

"Let's ring them now," I said, "before we get there and find the last three beds have been taken by some lecturers from Milton Keynes."

I have nothing against lecturers. Or Milton Keynes. But in that moment, with every fibre of my saturated being, I knew this: I would have wrestled them all to the death for a dry bed. I'd have taken them down with a soggy sock and a tent pole if necessary.

I meant it, too.

I was hoping Robin would nobly take the lead and pull out his phone to ring Kip in the Kirk, but instead, both he and Chris just turned to look at me with the blank expressions of men who had fully outsourced responsibility for basic decision-making. I sighed the sigh of the unfairly burdened and reached for my own phone, only to discover that my fingers didn't work.

They weren't just cold—they were in that concerning, borderline-unusable state where you start wondering if you're still technically alive. I wiggled them a bit to confirm I still had circulation and made a mental note to worry properly about it later.

Didn't matter anyway. No signal. Of course.

Rob, seeing my tech-based despair, produced his phone like a man revealing a rare and magical artefact. I read the number from the card we'd picked up earlier, and to his credit, he dialled it without fuss—then, rather more dramatically, handed the phone *back* to me, like he was passing the One Ring to Frodo.

The line rang once before a warm, friendly voice answered. Frances—the proprietor of Kip in the Kirk. Time to turn on the charm.

I slipped into my finest Phone Voice—posh, polite, and only mildly desperate—and explained that we were three idiotic Englishmen attempting to *swim* the West Highland Way and wondered if she had room for three dangerously damp morons who had made a series of appallingly bad decisions.

Frances, to her credit, didn't laugh. Not audibly, anyway. She said she hadn't thought *anyone* would be out walking today—which, translated from hospitality-speak, clearly meant, *"No sane human would be doing what you're doing."* Still, she was diplomatic about it, and more importantly, she had space for us.

Three morons: officially booked.

She gave us directions, which I half-listened to while trying to remember how to operate my limbs, and we promised to see her in about an hour. We all stood completely still during the entire conversation, like we were in a school play and the narrator was speaking. Only later did it strike me that we could have, I don't know, *kept walking*. They're called *mobile* phones for a reason.

Robin, who had boldly chosen shorts over waterproof trousers—presumably to prove a point to the universe—mentioned that his boots were now filling up from the top, like little portable bathtubs. Chris, who like me had gone Full Waterproof, reported that it had made absolutely no difference whatsoever. His boots were also waterlogged, his coat was clinging to him like a wet tent, and his morale was circling the drain.

At least I wasn't alone. Misery loves company, and our boots were squelching in perfect unison, a sort of soggy percussion line to accompany our march of despair. My so-called waterproofs had given up long ago, and by now were merely holding the water *in*, like a wet suit made of treachery.

Still, onward we sploshed. We passed an honesty box at Gartness, which on any other day might have been a charming little stop—but today we were too far gone for charm. It offered water, which felt deeply ironic. If there was one thing we didn't need more of, it was *that*.

The road twisted, climbed, and bent like a scenic fever dream, but as the height increased, so too did the view. For the first time in hours, we could see beyond the edge of our hoods. Rolling hills, distant lochs, and grey skies as far as the eye could squint. And then, like reaching a new level in a video game, we officially entered *Loch Lomond and the Trossachs National Park*—the full, proper title delivered by a sign so formal it almost needed a trumpet fanfare.

We had arrived. Wet, slightly broken, but technically victorious.

The rain, as if trying to outdo itself, somehow got even heavier. By now, it wasn't so much *falling* as *attacking*. We struggled on, grimly trudging forward like extras in a war film where the true enemy is Scottish weather. My fingers were trembling, my feet were absolutely sodden, and cold water once again found its favourite route down my spine. Rob and Chris looked equally destroyed, though no one was really speaking anymore. We'd moved past conversation and into that shared silence of people who have accepted their fate.

To the south, we could just about make out the Campsie Fells through the drizzle curtain. To the north, Conic Hill loomed—one of the better-known landmarks of the West Highland Way, and something I might have appreciated more if I hadn't been partially dissolved.

But all thoughts of scenery had vanished. Our entire mental focus was now locked on one thing: *Drymen*. And, more importantly, *Kip in the Kirk*.

We knew we were getting close when we passed Drymen Campsite, which gave us a brief flutter of hope—until we realised the actual village was still over a mile away. This final leg of the day was done in what I can only describe as sulky silence. We'd each reached that point of emotional fatigue where your soul just sort of sighs internally. The sight of several miserable campers trying to stay dry in a dripping barn did nothing to help our morale. It was like walking past a post-apocalyptic community theatre—everyone trying to pretend things weren't awful when everything clearly was.

And no matter *how* Drymen is pronounced (*Drimmen*, *Dry-men*, or *Drowned-men*), by the time we finally shuffled into the village, we were about as far from being dry as it's possible to be without developing gills. But then… salvation. We spotted the Kirk in the distance.

Our spirits lifted ever so slightly. Chris even managed to extract his camera from some hidden waterproof cavern to document what we looked like after a full day of recreational submersion. I smiled—or tried to—but mostly I just looked forward to peeling off my wet clothing, which by now resembled cold clingfilm more than actual fabric.

I rang the bell.

Nothing.

We stood there, dripping in perfect unison, wondering if we were about to be left outside to die like lost dogs. There was a moment where I genuinely considered whether Frances had seen us from the window and thought, *Nope. Absolutely not. I am not letting those three biological puddles into my nice clean guesthouse.*

I rang again, with the sort of hesitant dread usually reserved for pressing the red button on unlabelled machinery.

A faint voice responded, and suddenly the door swung open. "Come on in!" said a voice that sounded, in that moment, like it had been sent directly from heaven. We stepped inside, shutting the door behind us with the kind of reverence usually reserved for church doors or nuclear bunkers.

"Get out of those wet clothes and come straight through," said Frances, which was far easier said than done. Our fingers had long since abandoned the concept of dexterity. Chris, poor sod, was in such a bad state that Frances actually had to help him remove his backpack and waterproofs. Later, we'd joke that she leapt on him like some kind of rainwear-removing ninja, but at the time, no one was in the mood for comedy. We were in survival mode.

We dumped our dripping gear in the foyer like three molting sea lions and followed Frances into the main room.

Central heating.

Actual, blessed, real-life central heating.

And this was only the beginning. The place was immaculate—so pristine, in fact, that I briefly worried we might lower the property value just by existing inside it. But then came the kettle. Mugs of steaming tea were passed into our frostbitten hands. Then, as if in a slow-motion dream sequence, hot scones arrived. With jam. And butter.

I don't think I'm exaggerating when I say we believed we had died and gone to heaven. Or, at the very least, a particularly warm and well-catered version of purgatory. I honestly began to wonder whether our cold, drowned bodies were still lying along the path somewhere, like waterlogged breadcrumbs, and we were now just ghosts—doomed to haunt the West Highland Way, forever seeking shelter and baked goods.

But if this *was* the afterlife, it wasn't too bad at all.

Other walkers were staying at the Kirk too,

though in a different part of the building—presumably to avoid direct contamination by the three soggy disasters that had just flopped through the door. Frances asked if we'd mind them joining us in the kitchen, and it was clear she felt obliged to ask because of the pandemic, even though we all now existed in one great communal puddle. We had no objection whatsoever. And clearly, neither did they, because within minutes they were seated around the table, cheerfully joining us for tea and scones like we were all lifelong friends reunited after a tragic ferry accident.

There were four of them, all Scottish, all walking the West Highland Way, and all—let's be honest here—*much more professional-looking* than us. They had the calm, efficient air of seasoned trekkers. The sort who check the weather, plan ahead, and probably pack midge repellent and functional optimism.

Crucially, they were not carrying their own packs. No, they were using a luggage courier service to move their gear between stops, while we had chosen to carry ours like beasts of burden in a low-budget medieval re-enactment. To add insult to injury, they had started that same morning from Milngavie—three hours before us—and had already walked *past* Drymen and on to Balmaha before deciding to come back here for the night.

We had planned to do exactly the same—push on to Balmaha—to reduce the next day's mileage.

But, of course, the weather had other plans. Or more specifically, the weather had decided to punch us all directly in the morale.

The logic behind pushing on was sound: from Balmaha northwards, there's a huge area where wild camping is restricted. Too many people had treated the lochside like a personal landfill—leaving scorched earth from disposable barbecues, cans scattered like modern art, and in some truly classy cases, human poop. So, to avoid contributing to that or being caught short, the trick was to get past the camping ban zone on day two. Which meant pushing hard on day one.

Except we hadn't pushed. We'd floundered. But now we were dry, indoors, and possibly still alive, so frankly, we had no regrets.

As the kettle boiled once again, conversation flowed. Frances brought over a fresh pot of tea, which we all welcomed with the reverence normally reserved for relics or defibrillators. Unfortunately, one of the Scottish lads—Barrie—was a little *too* enthusiastic in his gratitude. In an effort to pour another cuppa, he lifted the teapot skyward, apparently unaware it had already emptied. Physics intervened. The lid clattered onto the table and shattered with a sense of finality usually reserved for ancient heirlooms in period dramas.

The room froze.

Frances leapt forward with the reflexes of a ninja who'd just seen a Fabergé egg hit the floor. "I've had that for *years*," she said, cradling what remained of her treasured teapot. Barrie looked absolutely mortified—like he'd just knocked over the Queen's corgi and reversed over her handbag.

Then, bizarrely, everyone started laughing. Why, I have no idea. It may have been hysteria. The kind of laughter that only happens after near-death experiences, emotional breakdowns, or being rained on sideways for five hours and realising your waterproofs are about as effective as tissue paper.

But here's the best part: the teapot became *famous*. That evening, I posted on the West Highland Way Facebook group about our hellish hike and the tragic demise of the beloved teapot. What happened next was truly unexpected: people began posting their *own* photos with *that* teapot. Stories. Memories. Tributes. It turned out we'd stumbled into a sort of unofficial cult of the Kirk Teapot. It was heartwarming. And also a bit weird.

Frances was nothing short of extraordinary that night. She washed and dried our clothes, helped us begin the delicate process of drying our boots (which were now classified as amphibious), and generally mothered us back into human form. Once we'd showered and regained the ability to bend our fingers, we felt semi-human again.

We went to bed warm, clean, and well-fed, all quietly pondering what on earth would've happened to us had we not made it to the Kirk. Outside, the wind howled wildly. Rain pelted the windows like an audition for *The Day After Tomorrow: Loch Lomond Edition*. We listened to it hammering the roof and realised just how lucky we were.

If we'd stuck to the plan and tried to camp, we wouldn't have been drifting off to sleep in comfy beds—we'd be in hospital. Or hypothermic. Or, more likely, clinging to a tree stump somewhere, trying to fight off pneumonia with a cereal bar.

Kip in the Kirk hadn't just saved the day.

It might've saved *us*.

Drymen To Rowchoish

If you don't like Scottish weather, just wait thirty minutes.

Everyone

Frances laughed when we told her we were aiming for Rowchoish Bothy today. Not a polite little chuckle either — a full, knowing guffaw from someone who had clearly seen many a hopeful walker disappear into the forest, never to be heard from again. And to be fair, she should know. She's lived here for thirty years, walked the West Highland Way more times than she's had hot dinners, and once even *ran* the bloody thing, presumably to flee a swarm of midges.

But we were undeterred. We left the Kirk feeling positively radiant — warm, dry, well-fed and fully convinced we could conquer Rowchoish, mostly because doing so meant we wouldn't have to faff about putting the tent up. Priorities. Call it laziness, call it tactical sloth — either way, a roof is a roof.

Before leaving Drymen, though, I had one

critical mission: Compeed. I'd somehow forgotten to stock up back in Milngavie, a mistake akin to heading into Mordor without a decent pair of socks. My feet were already protesting, and while I had a couple of those little blister-plaster miracles in my bag, I wasn't about to risk running out. That stuff is like gold dust wrapped in medical-grade magic.

If you've never used Compeed, then let me enlighten you. It's the blister equivalent of duct tape crossed with fairy dust. I've tried every brand going — even Elastoplast, which, fun fact, was invented in Hull (yes, *that* Hull) — and nothing sticks like Compeed. Apply it properly to dry feet and it'll hold through a monsoon, an avalanche, and possibly the apocalypse. I'm not being paid to say this — although frankly, I should be — but Compeed is the unsung hero of modern civilisation.

So, off I trotted to the local shop on the corner, hope in my heart and blisters on my feet. I asked the woman behind the counter if they had any. She looked at me through a large Perspex sheet — probably a leftover from pandemic times, or maybe she just didn't like the look of me — and blinked slowly, as if trying to decipher whether I'd asked for a medical supply or attempted to curse her in Latin.

Eventually, she explained that they'd thrown all the Compeed out. Binned it. Just like that.

Apparently, it had all gone out of date during lockdown, and since then they hadn't bothered restocking, not being sure when the walkers would return. I didn't even have to say a word — she clocked the rising fury in my eyes and started scribbling "compeed" onto a scrap of paper with the urgency of someone who'd just remembered they'd left the oven on. So that was something, at least. Future walkers: you're welcome.

I returned to the Kirk empty-handed but blister-aware, and off we went, wrapped once again in full waterproof gear, just in case the sky decided to spit on us again. Spoiler: it did.

The other guests had already left about half an hour before, and we nearly tripped over their luggage, which had been neatly arranged outside for some poor courier to haul off to Inverarnan. They'd mentioned they were walking from Balmaha, which was admittedly a decent trek, but considering they weren't carrying heavy packs, I reckoned it was doable — if not actually enjoyable.

We paid our dues, bid a fond farewell to Frances (who still looked amused by our bothy ambitions), and headed out east, right on cue for the drizzle to start again. Not quite the biblical downpour of the day before, more of a light moistening. Scotland's idea of mercy.

A brief shuffle along the road took us to a left turn up a wide track flanked by gorse in full, glorious bloom. It looked like the countryside had exploded in yellow confetti. I paused to take a photo, mostly because I was already knackered, and noticed how busy the trail was. Thanks to the long, straight path, we could see three separate groups of hikers ahead of us, all at different stages of the hill. It was like a walking-themed time-lapse.

Robin and Chris surged ahead like they'd been training for this moment their whole lives, and I was quickly left to puff my way up behind them. As I passed the first group — three women out for what looked like a cheerful wander — we exchanged the obligatory "Hiya" and "Morning!" like we were all pretending this was a pleasant day out and not some weirdly soggy purgatory.

Just as I tried to speed up, I felt a sudden twang in my lower left leg. Brilliant. Slowed me right down again, which meant the cheery trio ended up practically on my heels. Nothing like being tailgated uphill while you're nursing a limp and trying to look like you're not dying inside.

Eventually I caught up with the lads where the trail joined a broad logging track, and we paused for photos. We'd climbed a fair way and were now high enough to feel mildly heroic — or at least like we might deserve a biscuit. Not long after that, we caught our first glimpse of Loch Lomond, glittering in the distance like a smug reminder of how far we still had to go. We'd be walking along that loch for the rest of the day... and, oh joy, most of tomorrow too.

We reached a car park and found ourselves chatting with another group of women — the same ones who'd been miles ahead of us earlier. Turned out they'd paused for a snack, although "snack" might not be the right word. My jaw practically unhinged when one of them pulled out a hip flask and passed it around like they were in the final act of *Little Women*. Five o'clock somewhere? More like five miles into the woods, don't judge us. They offered us a swig, and while I usually jump at the chance to engage in some woodland whisky diplomacy, it still felt a bit early to start losing motor control. I had enough trouble staying upright as it was.

We plodded on through the forest, which was finally starting to behave itself. Sunlight broke through the canopy for the first time that day, a golden reminder that Scotland does occasionally remember how to summer. I spotted Rob and Chris up ahead, dropping their packs like two men auditioning for a very niche luggage advertisement. I caught up just as they were stripping off their waterproofs, and followed suit, figuring anything falling from the sky now would be more of a light blessing than a soaking. It felt daring. Practically tropical.

The path twisted, turned, dipped, rose, and generally behaved like it had something to prove.

As the sun climbed higher, I found myself genuinely appreciating the shade. And then — miracle of miracles — I realised I was actually *enjoying* the walk. Not just tolerating it, or surviving it, or mentally drafting my will, but properly enjoying it. Take that, Day One.

The lads would occasionally pause to let me catch up, then promptly vanish again the moment I appeared. Like woodland ghosts in breathable Gore-Tex. My pace had slowed, my leg was still twinging, and I was now entering that phase of the hike where the brain drifts off into soft, useless thoughts.

I daydreamed. Wondered what my wife was up to — probably pottering about the house and revelling in the blissful silence. The kids would be at school, unless they'd successfully staged a coup and were now running the place. I had briefly imagined bringing one of the dogs along, until I remembered that one's old and the other's basically a rat with ideas above its station. Ninety-six miles to either would feel like a trans-continental expedition.

I was snapped out of this reverie by the sight of Rob and Chris standing by a signpost up ahead, looking thoroughly confused. The sign pointed to Balmaha in *two* directions — left and right — like some sort of geographical prank. They looked ready to go left, so I shouted across the woods to ask where the pair of weaklings thought they were heading.

They conferred like lost Victorian explorers and replied they were going to Balmaha via Milton of Buchanan. Bless. I shook my head, marched up, and informed them in my best smug-know-it-all tone that Conic Hill is basically *the* landmark on this section of the West Highland Way. Missing it would be like visiting Paris and skipping the Eiffel Tower because the stairs looked a bit steep.

Now, to be fair, I *had* mentioned earlier that while the main Way skirts around the summit, there was a little spur if we wanted to go full mountaineer and bag it properly. Neither of them had been too fussed — the views were similar either way, and they'd rather not waste energy on vertical nonsense. The problem was, they thought *this* path was the detour. It wasn't. This *was* the Way. So off we went, up towards the infamous Conic Hill — with me loudly calling them pansies and various unprintables just to make sure the surrounding wildlife knew who was in charge.

A young couple nearby overheard the whole exchange and started laughing. I explained the situation: my friends had tried to take the easy way out, and I was here to shame them back into the righteous path of effort and Instagrammable vistas. We left the couple at a gate where they were busy excavating their bags for snacks, although in hindsight I suspect they were also planning to sneak down the shortcut once we were out of sight. You can always spot fellow cowards. It's in the eyes.

As we climbed, I commented how weirdly dry the trail was — especially considering we'd spent the previous day being slowly poached in our waterproofs. I figured it was down to a combination of elevation, strong drainage, and the type of wind that could skin a sheep.

Robin looked around at the forestry and made a note-to-self observation that he now knew where to come for a Christmas tree. I agreed, although I pointed out the small logistical detail of the six-hundred-mile round trip, the £100 fuel bill, and the five-mile hike required to drag a tree out of the wilderness like some kind of Yuletide lumberjack. After a moment of reflection, Rob muttered one word. Asda.

As the trees began to thin and the looming lump of Conic Hill emerged in full, imposing glory ahead of me, I realised — yet again — I was on my own. Robin and Chris had vanished, off chasing views or possibly just trying to avoid any more tree-based banter. All I could hear was the wind whispering through the treetops and birds singing like they had something to prove.

Rounding a corner, I spotted a large metal gate that marked the end of the woodland stretch. What I *didn't* spot was any sign of Rob and Chris. No figures on the moorland ahead. No sound of boots, conversation, or unnecessary commentary about trees. I hadn't heard a gate creak or bang. For a brief moment, I wondered if I'd taken a wrong turn — or perhaps stumbled into one of those Scottish myths where people walk into a glen and disappear for a hundred years, only to return and find contactless payment has replaced cash.

Then I nearly died.

Not metaphorically. I mean *actual* heart-leaving-chest territory, because at that precise moment, Rob and Chris launched themselves out of a gorse bush, screaming like banshees. If their goal was to make me soil myself, they very nearly succeeded. Honestly, at my age, the surprise alone could've triggered a minor stroke. Had they been half a second louder, they'd have had to carry me down the hill in a bivvy bag.

I warned them. What goes around comes around. I told them to watch their backs — not just today, not just on the West Highland Way, but forever. One day I *will* get them back. Possibly with an air horn. Possibly in a tent. Possibly at 3am.

Once I'd managed to coax my heart rate back down into triple digits, we descended into a gulley and passed through a small patch of woodland that felt suspiciously like a setup for another ambush. Fortunately, the only thing lying in wait this time was the hill. And what a hill it was. The path to Conic Hill ramped up fast, and I took immense pleasure in overtaking Rob — who, as we've established, is a large unit and climbs like a wounded fridge.

I offered helpful motivational slogans as I passed him. "Come on, slowcoach!" "Is that *both* lungs wheezing, or just one?" "Old age creeps up fast, doesn't it?" I carried on up the slope chatting with Chris, loudly wondering what it must be like to have to wait for such a feeble companion.

Naturally, the joy didn't last long. Robin caught up on a flat bit and briefly surged ahead — a short-lived moment of glory I was all too happy to steal back the second the incline returned. Meanwhile, Chris remained ahead of both of us, prancing up the hill like a smug mountain goat.

At what felt like the summit — or at least the highest bit *we* were going to bother with — Chris stood waiting with a bag of Haribo, waving it like a reward for surviving a game show. I got there first, so I had first dibs. A solid couple of hours later, Rob finally rolled into view, doing his best impression of a steam engine about to explode.

With our sugar levels topped up and our thighs throbbing in protest, we took a few photos and admired the view. And what a view it was. Loch Lomond stretched endlessly into the distance, shimmering in that smug way water does when it knows it's prettier than you. Dotted across it were little islands, which — trivia alert — mark the Highland Boundary Fault, a giant geological scar separating the Highlands from the Lowlands. Those huge mountains to the north? They used to be part of the Appalachian range before Scotland broke off from North America around fifty million years ago. Yes, really.

So if bits of the Highlands look suspiciously like parts of the US northeast, now you know why. And if you're wondering why the Appalachian Trail now unofficially includes the West Highland Way, it's because a bunch of enthusiastic geologists couldn't resist the chance to create the world's least convenient through-hike. You're welcome.

I found myself wishing there'd been a sign explaining all this — you know, for the benefit of people who didn't have the spare brainpower to do a crash course in plate tectonics mid-walk. But maybe a big placard would've ruined the view. As it was, I only figured it all out later, probably while Googling "why does Loch Lomond look like a ripped map of Maine?"

We began the descent towards Balmaha, and it was immediately obvious that the path had suffered. It was steep, churned up, and eroded into something resembling a World War One trench system. Clearly, thousands of walkers had looked at the official trail and thought, *Nah, I'll just bomb it down this bit instead.* Unfortunately, so had everyone else. So the entire hillside had become one wide, confused mess of sliding feet and eroded shame. You couldn't even tell where the "real" path was supposed to be. You just sort of hoped for the best and tried not to break an ankle.

The crowds increased the lower we got. People were clearly out for a weekend hill jaunt from Balmaha, striding up with various levels of enthusiasm, clothing, and competence. The sun was now properly out, which helped distract from the fact that my knees were plotting a mutiny.

Halfway down, I exchanged greetings with a group of girls on their way up — or possibly on their way to a nightclub, judging by the state of their attire. One of them looked like she'd had an accident in a vat of orange emulsion. And before you accuse me of being unkind to strangers, let me assure you: I am equally savage to my own friends. Fair's fair. Besides, this particular shade of fluorescent terracotta was *deliberate*. I'm assuming it was fake tan — either that, or she'd recently escaped from Willy Wonka's spray booth.

The irony was, she was a very pretty girl and really didn't need to bathe herself in radioactive nectarines. But that's fashion for you — baffling, expensive, and usually sticky.

But all was not lost for our tangerine-hued hillwalker. She had one saving grace: nestled in her arms was a tiny, trembling sausage dog. The sort that looks like it's been designed by someone who's only ever seen dogs described in vague sketches.

The poor little chap was whimpering softly, either because he didn't like heights or because he, too, was concerned about the unnatural glow of his human.

We got chatting. She was actually very pleasant — polite, friendly, and entirely unbothered by my presence, which was refreshing. She explained that she was turning around because she'd bitten off more than she could chew, and also, in her words, *Haggis didn't like it*. Yes. That was the dog's name. *Haggis*. I wish I could say I made that up, but no. I couldn't have invented a better name if I tried. A small tan dog named after Scotland's most divisive foodstuff.

She asked me if I was enjoying the walk. I told her it had its ups and downs. She nodded politely but didn't laugh. I don't think she quite got it — either the joke or the entire idea of walking for fun.

Anyway, I left the luminous lass and her trembling meat tube behind and caught up with Robin and Chris near a small gate built into a stone wall — the kind of gate that suggests you're about to enter either a forest or a legally grey area. A nearby sign helpfully declared that wild camping beyond this point was strictly forbidden and would result in a £500 fine, public flogging, and possibly being catapulted back to Milngavie. Fair enough. That was the reason we were pressing on to Rowchoish Bothy — a sentence that sounds like you've just sneezed mid-sentence.

I *had* tried to get a permit for the local campsite, which was delightfully called *Lochan Maoil Dhuinne*, presumably invented by a committee of dyslexic bagpipers. But it was fully booked, and frankly, I could barely pronounce it without spraining a vowel. Rowchoish it was.

Chris had already slinked through the gate like a woodland ninja by the time I arrived. Robin, however, was performing a more dramatic routine, climbing the fence rails like a man trying to wrestle gravity into submission. Let's just say there was *some girth management* involved. Not to be unkind — I had to do the same. Middle age doesn't creep up on you, it drops from a great height and lands squarely on your core strength.

I reached up to get a good grip on the top rail, ready to heave myself through, and promptly grabbed a proud, rusty chunk of Scotland's finest vintage barbed wire. The scream that followed could've woken the Loch Ness Monster. I let go instantly, wedged myself inside the kissing gate like a particularly miserable sausage roll, and spent the next few seconds inventing new swear words.

Naturally, Robin and Chris did nothing. I'm convinced they were standing there laughing. I couldn't see them — my eyes were filled with tears and rage — but I *know* those two. If they weren't laughing, they were definitely taking pictures.

Eventually, I extricated myself from the kissing gate of doom, checking my hand for signs of tetanus, plague, or potential amputation. A small queue of walkers had gathered by this point, no doubt hoping for an encore performance. And yes, right at the front of the crowd were our favourite neon tourist and her dog Haggis, now watching me with a look that clearly said, *And you mocked me.* I could hear the universe laughing.

Muttering "nothing to see here, folks" like a disgraced circus clown, I shuffled off in shame. Rob and Chris were already ahead of me, naturally, probably posting the incident online with hashtags like #barbedwirefail and #kissinggatecasualty.

My leg had now progressed from "minor twinge" to "full-blown throbbing complaint." I made a mental note to slap on some painkillers and anti-inflammatory gel when we stopped for lunch — assuming I wasn't carted away by the wild camping police first.

The stop came soon enough. After a clumsy descent, a bustling car park, and a short wander through humanity, we arrived in Balmaha. It was packed. Proper tourist levels of packed. Souvenir shop queues, families with ice creams, confused-looking men holding folded maps upside-down — the works. Among them were the hip-flask ladies from earlier, now very much rehydrated and lounging like queens.

Robin, ever the diplomat, asked them if they'd taken the easy route. They replied, "Absolutely," with the sort of tone that managed to sound both proud *and* aggressive. "No shame in that," they added, which of course is the international code for "We absolutely know there's shame in this, and we don't care." I smiled and nodded politely. Internally, I agreed. There's no shame in taking the easy way out — *if you're a bunch of pansies.*

We collapsed — quite literally — onto the nearest bench outside the Oak Tree Inn. We didn't really have a choice. Just before it, a sign cheerily pointed left with the word "Pub" and promised *safety*. If we'd carried on north, apparently there were *bears*. Not metaphorical ones either — it said *bears*, as in large, clawed woodland nightmares. Frankly, given the choice between *beers* or *bears*, there is only ever one correct answer. And if you picked bears, please stop reading this and go have a word with yourself.

So, we flopped at the table and looked at the laminated instructions for how to order a drink — because in the post-COVID age, getting a pint requires a degree in computer science and the patience of a monk. We didn't want food. Just a drink. Just a lovely cold pint. But no — we had to scan a QR code, order online, pay with plastic, offer a blood sample and maybe sacrifice a goat. Or at least that's how it felt.

Unfortunately, I hadn't brought my bank card,

which meant Chris had to foot the bill. Now, watching Chris try to get the app working was like watching a man try to programme a microwave using only his elbows. He scanned the code. Nothing. Scanned again. Still nothing. He was one failed attempt away from punting his phone into Loch Lomond when, finally, it worked. Then came the multi-page menu, then the payment screen, and just as he got to the final hurdle... it crashed.

He let loose a string of expletives that probably made the trees blush, and started all over again. This time, it worked — until he was asked to choose *which beer garden* he was in. Front? Rear? Side? Upper? Lower? Diagonal? Quantum realm? We had no idea. It was like the bloody Crystal Maze out here. Luckily, a waitress emerged with someone else's order and took pity on us. We asked her which beer garden we were in and she said, with the weariness of someone who answers this question 48 times a day, "Front-right-lower-side-second-from-left-back-to-front."

She then gave us a look. You know the one. The look that says, *Oh. You're English*. As if that explained everything. Which, let's be fair, it probably did. And just to twist the knife, she added, "You could've just gone inside to the bar... if you had a mask." The look on Chris's face at this revelation could've curdled whisky.

Anyway, order finally placed, a message popped up on Chris's phone saying our drinks would arrive sometime in the next 48 hours. Brilliant. So, with morale now somewhere between "low" and "I'll just lie down in the loch," I went off to explore.

Opposite the pub I found something intriguing — a mysterious box with a handle. Naturally, I turned the handle. Nothing happened. I turned it again. Still nothing. Then a gruff voice which sounded suspiciously like Robin said, "Turn it like a man if you want to hear the story."

Challenge accepted.

I gave it some welly, and the box began to speak. Rob Roy, it declared, is often referred to as Scotland's Robin Hood — which is largely thanks to Sir Walter Scott, who took one look at a violent ginger cattle thief and decided, "Yes, this man should be romanticised forever."

Roy was probably born around here, though what *is* certain is that he was baptised at Buchanan, just east of Balmaha. From there, he embarked on a lifelong career of stealing, feuding, escaping from things, and generally being a nuisance to everyone — especially the Duke of Montrose, who he hated with the fiery intensity of a thousand suns.

At one point, he was imprisoned by George I — who, in an unexpected twist, read Daniel Defoe's *Highland Rogue*, decided Rob sounded like a decent bloke, and gave him a royal pardon. It's the 18th-century equivalent of being released from prison because your Amazon biography had good reviews.

He's buried in Balquhidder, near Loch Voil — somewhere we'd be vaguely heading in the next century or so, if my leg didn't drop off first. I found it all thoroughly fascinating, but when I returned and told Rob and Chris, Rob was on his phone and Chris scratched his ear and yawned. I'm not the most intuitive soul, but I took that as a hint they didn't care. Fair enough. I shut up and sipped my pint.

Well, *necked* my pint, more like. We all did. And with beer now inside us, we stood up and — in a moment of wildly misplaced optimism — decided to ditch our waterproofs. We took three steps and the sky immediately opened again. Honestly, I think Scottish weather is run by someone with a remote control and a wicked sense of humour.

So, we stopped and begrudgingly pulled it all back on. It was then I spotted a statue nearby and called the others over. We're all suckers for a good statue.

And this one was a belter — Tom Weir, sporting his trademark woolly hat and surrounded by flowers. A local legend. A conservationist, broadcaster, mountaineer, writer, and all-around outdoorsy polymath. The man made hiking look cool long before Instagram filters did.

He travelled the world — Greenland, the

Himalayas, North Africa — but his true love was always Scotland. In the 1970s, he starred in *Weir's Way*, a TV series that saw him tramp around the country talking to local folk about hills, lochs, peat bogs, and how midges were invented by the devil. He passed away in 2006, and this statue was erected in 2014 as a tribute to everything he did for nature, Scotland, and good hat fashion.

We stood next to him, took a photo, and tried — briefly — to channel his spirit.

Then, naturally, we buggered off into the woods again like lost schoolboys.

Leaving Tom Weir behind — as stoic and statue-still as ever — we carried on our way. The path turned off the road near a small white cottage, which was a relief because the alternative was a road climb that looked like it had been designed by someone who *hated* knees. A sign pointed helpfully to Rowardennan up the road, but also warned drivers about a 15% gradient. FIFTEEN. That's not a road, that's a vehicular death wish. There was even a note, presumably aimed at rogue bus drivers, telling them not to even *think* about it. You know you're in trouble when the sign pre-empts your bad ideas and calls them out in advance.

So we took the off-road path instead, which promptly decided it too would like to be steep — just in a more rustic, ankle-twisting sort of way.

My leg started pulling again, worse than before, but I blamed the half-hour pub stop and the beer that had definitely lubricated *neither* joints nor motivation. Still, not too worried yet. Just sore. And increasingly grumpy.

At the top, we were treated to a glorious view over Balmaha and Loch Lomond — which a young couple had entirely failed to notice, being far too busy playing tonsil tennis. They were fully engaged in the sort of romantic entanglement that suggests their walk had ended several minutes ago, and their hormones had taken over the itinerary. We politely looked away, then less politely walked away. Good luck in nine months, I thought, with all the smugness of a man who'd just climbed a hill to witness someone else's biology lesson.

The descent was mercifully quick — proof that even cruel climbs have a use — and before long we were back at the loch's edge on a smooth, level gravel path. We were also now able to confirm, with great irritation, that we *could* have walked around the headland on a flat trail and skipped the whole hill entirely. Classic West Highland Way: go up something unpleasant for "views" and "character," then find out there was an easier option all along. Still, we'd have missed the view — and the forest flirtation session — so I suppose we were richer for the trauma.

The lochside path started strong but quickly

fell into its usual tricks. It narrowed, sprouted tree roots like nature's tripwires, and offered low-hanging branches positioned *perfectly* to hit either your face or your groin, depending on your height and luck. It was less of a hike and more of a never-ending game of dodge-the-dendrology.

Robin and Chris powered on ahead, because apparently they have some sort of unspoken competition to see who can get to Rowchoish first and claim the good sleeping spot. I hobbled along in the rear, increasingly aware that my leg now had opinions and none of them were good.

Far ahead, I could just make out the moment the lads caught up with that group of older ladies we'd seen earlier — the ones who'd sensibly opted out of Conic Hill and probably enjoyed a latte while we were wrestling barbed wire. There was a brief exchange between them, though I couldn't hear the words. Until I could.

By the time I caught up, I was just in range to hear one of the ladies — silver hair, hiking poles, and the aura of someone who's survived multiple marriages — say in a stage whisper, "There are five of us and only two of them. We could just grab them and chuck them in our tent."

It was at this exact moment that she noticed me walking silently up behind them like a sweaty ninja.

"Are you with them?" she asked, cheeks

suddenly crimson.

"With them?" I said, raising an eyebrow and grinning like a man who'd just caught his nan Googling "how to tie up hikers." "Oh yes. Most definitely."

Her embarrassment was magnificent. She turned so red I feared for her blood pressure. The grin on my face, however, only got wider.

They were all good fun, in the end. No one tried to drag me into their tent (disappointing, in a way), and I ended up walking with them for about a mile. They were charming, cheerful, and slightly too interested in gin for 2pm. I learned that yes, they all worked together; no, they weren't camping (don't be silly); and of course they weren't carrying their own bags — they'd left that to some poor courier.

One of them came from Blackburn, all of them had opinions about every man they'd ever met, and they were heading to Rowardennan, probably with plans to drink it dry.

I left the gin-loving grannies behind as we approached Milarrochy Bay Campsite, where Rob and Chris were standing patiently, looking like a pair of disappointed dads waiting for their lost child to emerge from a soft play centre. I explained that my leg pain had now graduated from "minor twinge" to "genuinely inconvenient," and that they should probably go on without me. I'd just lie down somewhere scenic and spend my remaining days in the woods like some sort of middle-aged Scottish hermit. They refused, of course — not out of loyalty or friendship, but because I was carrying *part of the tent*. The dead weight they could live without. The flysheet? Not so much.

Milarrochy Bay was rather lovely, actually. Neat little pitches dotted the shore of the loch, and I imagined the sort of stunning sunrise you might witness here on a clear morning — which is to say, once every four years, if you're lucky, because *Scotland*. Still, it had charm. As I hobbled along the shoreline, I somehow ended up in front of Rob and Chris, which meant I was now the leader. This, naturally, meant we were soon lost.

The path, as it turns out, *should* have followed the road. But I had decided that the loch shore was more pleasant — and it was — so we ignored the trail and stuck to the rocks. That rebellious detour paid off when I stumbled across a lone tree, looking like it had walked out of a travel brochure and stood itself on the lochside just to be photographed. Apparently, it's one of the most photographed trees in Scotland. I could've made a sarcastic comment here, but I won't. Because — whisper it — it really *was* quite beautiful. But let's keep that between us. I've got a reputation to maintain.

Eventually, the terrain forced us back to the official route, which led us through the village on the road — a route that missed *all* the good bits, naturally. Just a couple of houses, a campsite, and a sense of missed opportunity. Still, we were walking together for once — a rare and almost unsettling moment of unity. We used it to agree that today was far better than yesterday. Mostly because we were walking, not swimming.

A brief flirtation with lochside bliss was swiftly yanked away as the path cruelly crossed the road and plunged us once again under a thick green canopy. You know the sort — leafy, shady, full of scenic promise and hidden inclines. The trail twisted and rose, dipped and turned, and offered us occasional glimpses of the mighty Ben Lomond through the clearings. Real name: Beinn Laomainn. It's the most southerly of Scotland's Munros — and apparently very proud of it.

A Munro, as you may recall (and if not, congratulations on having a life), is any Scottish mountain over 3,000 feet. And for reasons no one can fully explain, people try to climb *all* of them. This hobby is known as Munro bagging, which involves ticking off as many as you can before your knees give out or your loved ones leave you. There are 282 in total. That's not a hill list. That's a cry for help.

Ben Lomond, despite its towering presence from down here, ranks a measly 182nd in height. That's right — *181* mountains in Scotland are bigger than this absolute unit. Which tells you everything you need to know about Scottish geography and nothing about Scottish humility.

Now technically — and I mean *technically* — I've already started Munro bagging. I've been to the top of Ben Nevis, Scotland's tallest, and also Ben Lomond. Admittedly both were in my youth, back when joints still worked and I didn't creak when standing up. I didn't "bag" them, though. I just wandered up like an idiot without a spreadsheet or an Instagram post. I'll leave the proper bagging to people with stronger knees and lower standards for leisure.

Eventually, and quite without warning, the trail burped us out onto the road again — just in time to follow it a few hundred yards to Cashel Campsite. This bit of road walking was thankfully separated from traffic, because while the road's a dead end, it was somehow still busier than the M8. I was grateful for the barrier between me and any stray campervan doing 40.

Cashel itself was a bit of a non-event. Perfectly pleasant, I'm sure, if you were staying there — which we weren't — so we breezed through, nodded at a few tents, and carried on. The path now stuck close to the road but for some inexplicable reason insisted on bouncing up and down like a kid on a sugar high, despite the road itself being flatter than a squashed midge. Every single undulation stabbed at my shin like it had a personal grudge.

For a fleeting moment, I considered ditching the trail and just walking along the road instead. And then a truck — a *massive* one, loaded with gas canisters and going at a speed better suited to Formula One — came thundering around a bend and reminded me why that was a *terrible* idea. I had no desire to become a cautionary tale smeared across a verge.

So I kept trudging. My leg now felt like it was auditioning for a role in *Casualty*. Rob and Chris, fuelled by caffeine, spite, or both, had galloped ahead, leaving me wobbling in their wake. I caught up with them at Anchorage Cottage, a lovely old white building perched perfectly on the loch's edge, looking like it had just stepped out of a VisitScotland brochure. We leaned on a perfectly placed stone wall, just the right height to prop up our backpacks and our spirits.

I told them I'd be slowing down a bit. Rob laughed and said I was already *permanently* slow — that if I went any slower, I'd start going backwards. Chris chuckled, and I limped on, wondering if there was an award for Most Sarcastically Abused Walker. If there is, I want it engraved.

After another long, straight stretch up a gentle incline, the trail once again veered off the road and into the woods — with one final piece of bureaucratic madness to send us on our way. A sign announced, proudly and without irony, that *your council is now in charge of parking fines*. I stared at it, blinking in confusion. *My* council? *Hull City Council*? What in the name of all that is holy was Hull doing policing car parks in remotest Scotland? Had they annexed Loch Lomond while nobody was looking? Were they planning to extend the Number 57 bus service all the way to Ben Nevis?

Shaking my head at this logistical sorcery, we continued into the woods, where Sallochy Bay appeared through the trees like a Highland postcard — picnic tables, lakeside views, and just enough midges to remind you who's boss. It was a beautiful spot, and we took the opportunity to ditch our packs, scoff chocolate and Haribos, and pretend we weren't in any physical distress. The picnic tables were even kitted out with special barbecue stands, which someone had obviously ignored, choosing instead to char the actual wood. Humanity, ladies and gentlemen.

As we sat recovering, three girls we'd last seen back at the Oak Tree wandered by. They were heading for Rowardennan and waved with the casual cheerfulness of people who hadn't just had an intimate conversation with a barbed-wire fence. I told them to get the drinks in for when we caught up, and they laughed. I wasn't joking.

Unfortunately, our peaceful moment was shattered by the arrival of yet another rain shower — because of course it was. With a collective groan, we shrugged back into our wet gear and hoisted our packs again.

My leg had now entered its *dramatic* phase —
each step on the flat sent twinges ripping through
it, whereas going uphill weirdly didn't hurt at all.
Downhill was tolerable. So really, I was now in
favour of mountains. Just not... Scotland's version
of "flat."

Still, middle of nowhere, no taxi rank in sight
— I followed my friends and hobbled on. So when
the trail decided to throw a massive hill at us right
after Sallochy, I was *delighted*. Genuinely pleased. I
powered up it like a man whose knee had forgotten
it was angry, while the path resumed its usual
party trick of twisting and dipping like a drunken
conga line.

More views of Ben Lomond offered periodic
distractions, and I tried to follow our progress on
the map. I failed. The only point where I had any
real idea where we were was when we came to
some duckboards across swampy ground. Because
when you're wading through marsh on wooden
planks, you *know* where you are: stuck.

Soon after, we were greeted by the charming
little Mill of Ross — a lovely whitewashed cottage
nestled into the trees, next to a rustic old barn that
looked like it hosted regular boot camps for mildly
traumatised teenagers. By this point, we'd fallen
into that forest-walking trance — the one where
the trees blur into one endless corridor and your

thoughts go a bit floaty.

Then — suddenly, like a pub-shaped jump scare — the Rowardennan Hotel *leapt* out at us. One moment it was all trees and trail, the next there was a full-blown building. Rain threatened again but, in an uncharacteristic act of mercy, decided not to bother. We collapsed at a picnic bench opposite the hotel and exhaled.

Just as we sat, who should reappear but our flirty middle-aged fan club — the ladies who'd once plotted to abduct Rob and Chris in their tent. They asked how we were doing. I replied with the classic British "Fine, how are you?" while silently wondering if I'd be able to stand up again without the aid of scaffolding.

They were going inside for chips, they said, which made Rob exclaim "Bloody hell" — not at the prospect of fried food, but because, out of nowhere, a massive military cargo plane appeared over the pub. It was flying so low it may have clipped someone's pint. It lumbered past us like a flying car park, engines howling, wings practically brushing the trees.

We all watched in stunned silence as it barely cleared the hotel roof, limped over the loch, and slowly curved northward. I half-expected it to explode, but no — it simply vanished into the Highland haze, presumably on a secret mission to scare hikers and confuse ducks.

Rowardennan, by the way, gets a literary shoutout in Sir Walter Scott's famous poem *The Lady of the Lake* — although he called it "Dennan's Row," presumably because he was writing with a quill and spellcheck hadn't been invented yet.

Once the ladies disappeared into the pub for their carbs and possibly more gin, we pressed on. Sort of. First, we had to make it out of the car park, and I managed to delay even *that* by turning myself into an impromptu comedy sketch.

We'd taken off our packs to give our backs a break, and I had the bright idea of using a picnic table to hoist mine on. So I set the pack on the table, turned around, slid my arms into the straps — and promptly tipped backwards like a flipping tortoise. One moment I was adjusting the waist belt, the next I was flat on my back on top of the table, limbs flailing, dignity gone, legs twitching in the air like a panicked beetle.

Rob and Chris did exactly what you'd expect: nothing helpful whatsoever. Instead, one of them whipped out a camera and shouted "Don't move!" as if I was mid-ballet. I lay there helpless while they laughed so hard I'm surprised they didn't pull a muscle. It felt less like hiking with adults and more like babysitting two overly mobile toddlers with access to smartphones.

Eventually, Robin showed some mercy and helped me up, and we waddled on through the car park, heading north. But no sooner had we moved fifty feet than the rain finally committed to its earlier threat and dumped a proper shower on us. Again.

Just beyond the picnic table debacle, we came across a large granite sculpture — a striking ring stood on its edge with a triangle shape embedded at the bottom, presumably representing Ben Lomond. It looked like some sort of modernist archway into the multiverse. A nearby plaque explained that it was a war memorial, honouring those who made the ultimate sacrifice in the world wars. And through its centre, as if nature had art-directed the scene herself, was the imposing snow-capped peak of Ben Vorlich — looming out of the mist and storm clouds like a Highland god. Say what you want about the weather — it knows how to frame a mountain.

Rain threatening again (because of course it was), we trudged on, once more zipped into our wet gear. I would like to point out, for the record, that about an hour later I realised said wet gear — the same jackets and trousers that had let me get utterly poached in yesterday's downpour — now seemed 100% effective at *trapping sweat*. It's as if Gore-Tex had suddenly reversed its allegiance and decided, "You know what? Let's just make him stew in his own juices."

There was supposed to be a shelter here with a water tap. I'd been liberal with my camel bag all day, assuming I'd refill it easily. But after a full-scale rummage of the shelter revealed not even the faintest glimmer of plumbing, we pressed on. Parched. Slightly betrayed. Probably a little stinkier.

But then — salvation. An honesty box. Glorious and unexpected, like a mirage but made of wood and snacks. We were drawn to it like moths to a flapjack. It was crammed with sweeties, crisps, juice boxes, and joy. Chris, being the only one carrying actual currency like it was 1999, got volunteered as our snack financier. I didn't tell him you could also pay through an app — because frankly, those coins were weighing him down. I was doing him a *service*, really.

Flapjack acquired, I gobbled mine immediately. Chris followed suit. Rob — ever the romantic — said he was saving his for later. *Not if I got to it first*, I thought, eyeing his pocket like a ravenous squirrel.

Then came the choice: continue on the wide, sensible forestry track like well-adjusted adults... or turn left onto the rugged shoreline trail, as recommended by masochists and guidebook writers with a grudge. I told Rob and Chris that only *pansies* took the fire road. Real men — and women — took the lochside path. The hard way. The true way. The route where boots go to die.

To their credit, they agreed. Rob had already

said, back on Conic Hill, that he was glad we hadn't wimped out and walked the road to Balmaha. I wanted to finish this walk knowing we hadn't cut corners — even if my leg was currently threatening to detach itself out of protest.

Almost instantly, the trail changed its personality entirely. Gone was the flat, friendly gravel. This was now a single-file slog over roots, rocks, puddles, and what I can only assume were relics from ancient Viking shipwrecks. Chris, the speed demon, led the charge. Rob followed. I hobbled along at the rear, limping like a pirate with one wooden leg and no sense of direction.

Every bend offered a new hazard — a slippery descent, a hidden tree root, a branch that tried to remove my hat. Occasionally, the trees parted to reveal the loch, sometimes directly below us in a manner that raised questions about health and safety. Then the path would dive back into the foliage like it was scared of being scenic for too long.

Every so often, I'd round a corner and find the others waiting for me. It was very touching. For about five seconds. Then they'd immediately vanish again, like forest phantoms. Every step was a stab of pain in my left leg, and I found myself dreaming of stopping. Not even camping — just *stopping*.

Finally, after about an hour of root-dodging

misery, I came over the crest of a small hill and saw them both up ahead, standing in a clearing. Without a word, I knew exactly what they were thinking. The spot looked *ideal* for a tent. Flat. Quiet. Hidden. Tempting.

But... no. No. Not here.

Now technically, wild camping is banned along much of Loch Lomond's shoreline due to it being a designated conservation area. I wasn't entirely sure if we'd passed the invisible "get fined here" line yet, but I *thought* we had — somewhere north of Ptarmigan Lodge. That wasn't really the point, though.

See, just around the corner was *Rowchoish Bothy* — and I wanted that bothy. I'd never stayed in one. Never done the full "rugged hut in the wilderness" experience. It was one of the few along the entire West Highland Way. And this? This was my chance.

There was another bothy further up the trail — Doune — but it was only eight miles from here, and stopping there tomorrow would be a bit of a waste. No, if I wanted a night in a proper Scottish bothy — a night of smoke-stained stone walls and wind howling through the gaps — this was it. This was the night.

Even with my leg screaming and my energy tank flashing empty, I wasn't about to camp in a clearing and miss out. I was finishing this day in

Rowchoish. If I had to crawl there using only my teeth and spite, so be it.

Repeating the mantra that it was *just around the corner*, we pressed on — each at our own pace, which in my case was somewhere between "injured hiker" and "heavily sedated tortoise." Rob and Chris waited for me a couple of times and kept asking how much farther the bothy was, since I had the guidebook. My stock response of "just around the corner" had, apparently, lost its charm. Now it just made them laugh like toddlers at a fart joke. Still, we carried on, corner after corner after increasingly soul-destroying corner.

Eventually — miraculously — after a series of brutal little ups and downs that seemed purpose-built to destroy my leg entirely, the path veered away from the loch. That was a good sign. A *very* good sign. I suddenly knew exactly where we were. I confidently announced, once again, that the bothy was just around the corner. Rob and Chris, rather unfairly I thought, erupted into actual guffaws.

But then — finally — a steep climb led us up past a moss-choked ruin on the left, slowly being devoured by the forest. A final left turn through the trees… and there it was.

Rowchoish Bothy.

We could smell wood smoke as we approached, which meant someone had beaten us to it. Frances, back at the Kirk, had told us we could camp on the grass outside if it was full. But that wasn't what concerned me. What *did* concern me was the remote possibility of walking into a damp murder shed in the middle of the woods and meeting an unhinged man wielding a splitting axe and some very strong opinions about hiker etiquette.

Still, I was now far too tired to care. My leg was in open revolt, my energy levels had dropped through the floor, and if someone wanted to chop me into firewood, I might've actually welcomed it.

Rob and Chris were already inside by the time I staggered up to the door. As I fumbled with the bolt, a deep, booming voice yelled, *"We're full!"*

It was just Rob. Being Rob.

I ignored him, opened the door, and stepped into what I can only describe as a slightly upgraded shed with smoke retention issues. There were already five people inside. I made six.

And here's a fun fact: if the bothy looks vaguely familiar to you, that's probably because it starred — yes, *starred* — in a BAFTA-nominated film a few years back. It featured none other than Scarlett Johansson in *Under the Skin*, a film that follows her as she roams around Glasgow and the Highlands seducing men, who she then, naturally, devours. Also, she's an alien. Because of course she is. It's arthouse.

Anyway, back in the real bothy, introductions

were made. Sort of. I immediately clocked which one was likely to be the murderer: the man asleep in the corner with two dogs, a huge bushy beard, a military-grade backpack, and a shiny new axe displayed beside him like it was on sale at B&Q. Now, I'm not saying he *was* a murderer, but if someone gets chopped in the night, I'm telling the police *exactly* who to look at first.

The other two occupants were much younger — mid-twenties, well-spoken, with just the right amount of smugness to suggest they had both read Proust and survived on quinoa. They'd built a roaring fire, which was admirable, although I suspected the chimney hadn't been swept since 1973, because the inside of the bothy now resembled a Cold War-era smokehouse.

My eyes began to stream — either from the dense smoke or the looming possibility of being butchered. I rubbed them, which naturally made everything ten times worse. I blinked through the haze to see Rob had already put the kettle on. Legend.

Backpack unloaded, I stood there feeling mildly useless. Everyone else seemed to know what they were doing, and I... didn't. Lacking any meaningful survival skills — or even *minorly* useful ones — I found a broom and started sweeping. Not because the floor needed it, really, but because I had definitely just tracked half of Loch Lomond's shoreline across the wooden platform, having failed to take my boots off like every other civilised human in the room.

So there I was: sore-legged, sweat-drenched, semi-blind from smoke, sweeping mud off a hut floor in the middle of nowhere with a possible axe murderer snoring behind me — and I couldn't have been happier.

I was in a bothy. And I'd earned it.

The bothy was a three-tier wonder. Just inside the door was the dirt floor — authentic, rustic, a touch *"early Bronze Age pit dwelling"*. A high step led up to the main living area, where a wooden platform held a table, a few chairs, and the all-important cooking space. Another step up again took you to the sleeping deck, where the axe-wielding forest troll still lay in the corner — only now, he had *one eye open*. Naturally. Because sleeping with both eyes closed is for people who *aren't* suspicious woodland cannibals.

At this point, I had upgraded his status in my mind from "potential axe murderer" to "probable cannibal," which sounds more alarming than it felt. Honestly, I was so tired, it was actually a comfort to remember that Robin had more meat on him. If someone was going to get slow-cooked in a cast-iron pan, it wasn't going to be me.

Then, just as I finished sweeping up and restoring my sense of contribution to society, Rob upended both of his boots directly onto my clean floor, scattering half of Loch Lomond across the platform. I stared at him. He smirked. I swept again, silently. Behind me, the madman licked his lips. So did his dogs. It was all very *comforting*.

Dinner was one of those delightful tinfoil pouches the army uses to convince soldiers they're being fed. Rob had the bright idea of combining *three* different flavours in one pan. The result was some sort of chicken–coconut–vague chemical surprise fusion that defied description but not hunger. It tasted like ration roulette — but I was too tired to care.

Coffee followed, and we finally started chatting to the others. The two well-spoken lads were taking the West Highland Way at a delightfully lazy pace, doing five miles a day and using the rest of their time to "do other things." Today's "other thing" had been fishing. I perked up — the thought of fresh trout sizzling on the fire was almost too good to be true.

And indeed, it was.

They hadn't caught a thing. "We're rubbish at it," they said, as if that made it better. I stared at them, trying to hide my crushed hopes behind a polite smile. I'd already mentally paired trout with my flapjack crumbs.

Our resident axe-wielding psychopath, meanwhile, turned out to be utterly lovely. Of course. Said he'd walked up to Fort William the week before and was now doing the return leg — as far as Balmaha, anyway. His wife was picking him up there. Casual, like. He said he wasn't bothering with the rest because he lived near Milngavie and found it "a bit boring." Fair enough. I mean, *we* thought it was stunning, but we were still West Highland Way virgins. He was clearly in the "been there, done that, eaten the tourists" stage.

Another coffee appeared, and I did the only decent thing and passed around my emergency Jack Daniel's — the universal hiker's nightcap. Then I decided it was time for the loo.

This, of course, is the one major downside of remote bothy life. While the scenery is spectacular and the company occasionally non-homicidal, there is *no toilet.* As my wife often reminds me, this is far less of a problem for men. Provided, of course, you don't require... anything technical. Fortunately, mine was a simple operation. Just a wee wander to a tree — far, far away from the bothy. Preferably one with no spectators. Luckily, the Highlands are well-stocked in tree departments.

Stepping outside, I expected darkness. We'd been inside for what felt like hours. But no — it was still broad daylight, or at least the Scottish summer version of it. I limped to my chosen tree, muttering obscenities under my breath about my leg, my bladder, and the concept of gravity, and made my peace with nature.

Back inside, I pocketed another one of Robin's anti-inflammatories, claimed a space on the sleeping platform, and prepared for the nightly concert of man-noises that inevitably comes with sharing a confined space with multiple bearded strangers. Rob's snoring, unsurprisingly, was the headline act. He was right next to me, of course — no escape there. I briefly considered strangling him with the drawstring from my parka hood, which is actually *perfect* for that kind of job. But I was too tired to carry out the murder. So instead, I rolled over and tried to imagine I was in a warm, fluffy, goose-stuffed sleeping bag instead of my cold nylon apology for one.

Sleep came. Eventually. Fitful, broken, but still better than no sleep at all.

Then came the footsteps.

A creak. A latch. A door opening.

Voices. Someone entering.

For a moment I thought, *Well, this is it. This is how I die. In a smoky hut in the woods, surrounded by strangers and gently poached in Gore-Tex.*

But no. It was just a man warming his hands by the dying fire. Didn't say a word. Just stood there. Then left again.

Chris, meanwhile, stood up — still inside his sleeping bag — and did a sort of child-in-a-sack-race hop across the platform to join Rob and me, making space for the mystery visitor. If you can picture a caterpillar doing a three-legged race, you've got the image.

The temperature dropped. I curled deeper into my bag, teeth chattering. I tried to think warm thoughts. Tried to visualise a nice down-filled sleeping bag... or better yet, a bin bag full of geese. Nothing worked.

I finally slipped into something resembling proper sleep — only to be jarred awake at 1 a.m. by a low-flying aircraft screaming overhead, followed by four distinct explosions. As you do. Then came the motorbikes — roaring through the forest like an off-road gang of vengeful spirits. It honestly felt like the climax to a very weird action film directed by someone with no sense of pacing.

After that? Blessed, uninterrupted sleep.

Well... for about two hours.

Rowchoish To Inversnaid

What doesn't kill you makes you stronger, apart from bears. They will kill you.

A funny guy.

It wasn't the daylight that woke me, but the telltale sounds of a sleeping bag being violently crammed into a compression sack, the hiss of a boiling kettle, and the low, half-whispered grumblings of other human beings—those awful morning types. I raised my head like a tortoise unsure if it was safe and realised that everyone else was already up, apart from Chris, who lay there like a corpse that snores.

I stretched dramatically, as if I'd spent the night heroically wrestling bears rather than whimpering into a nylon bag full of regret, and began the ritual of rolling up my sleeping bag. That's when I remembered a brilliant camping tip: you can easily compress your sleeping bag by running it over with your car. Unfortunately, my car was approximately a million painful steps away in Milngavie.

Standing up was a process. It was also freezing. Even though someone had coaxed the fire back to life, the place still had the air of a medieval cellar. I threw on my fleece and jacket, both of which now smelled like they'd been cold-smoked for six hours in a chimney designed by Satan. Still, on the bright side, I reasoned the midge population in my vicinity had probably been wiped out. Along with any bacteria, viruses, or wildlife within a ten-metre radius.

I turned to Rob and Chris, both now wide awake, and asked, quite casually, "So… did you hear the low-flying plane, the four explosions, and the motorbikes roaring through the woods like a travelling circus of the damned?"

They just stared at me.

"Er… no?" said Chris, with the kind of hesitant concern usually reserved for people on day release.

Rob frowned. "Are you sure that happened?"

And that's when it hit me — slowly, like a damp sock to the face.

Oh God.

The pill.

Maybe, just *maybe*, accepting random medication from someone whose qualifications include "owns a rucksack" wasn't my finest moment. For all I knew, I'd spent the night hallucinating air raids while high on expired horse tranquillisers. It's entirely possible I mistook a squirrel for a motorbike gang.

Lesson learned: never accept drugs from a man who snores like a dying yak and stores his painkillers in a sandwich bag.

Coffee was made and passed around like communion for the broken. The mad axeman complained—*vigorously*—about someone's snoring, and absolutely refused to believe us when we pointed to the actual culprit: Robin. The man who could saw through granite with his nose.

When the axe-man left, we all exhaled in collective relief. We weren't far behind. I took another painkiller for my leg, which was still staging a low-level rebellion. And with that, off we limped.

The short stagger back to the main path gave me a glimmer of hope. The pain in my leg had dulled slightly, and for about fifteen glorious seconds, I thought I might be fine. Of course, by the time I'd blinked, Robin and Chris were already tiny dots in the distance, and I was once again dragging myself behind them like a wounded war veteran on his last mission.

They paused about a hundred yards ahead to let me catch up, which I did with all the grace of a three-legged llama. I told them not to bother waiting every five minutes—I'd just catch them up when I could. This became our dynamic for the day: two fit lads up front, and me hobbling behind like a man with a boot full of Lego.

The path twisted and turned and behaved itself slightly better than the previous day, but it was still the kind of trail that made you question whether walking was really a good use of your time on Earth. Gaps in the trees teased us with gorgeous views across Loch Lomond and the snow-dusted mountains beyond. Beautiful, yes. But it was starting to feel like *Groundhog Loch*. How long *was* this lake? Were we even making progress or just trapped in some scenic loop?

After about an hour, I caught up to the others again and had to stop. Took the backpack off. Sat down. Looked like I'd just been rescued from a shipwreck. They looked at me with the pity usually reserved for injured labradors. Then Chris pulled out a bag of Haribos, and I briefly considered marrying him.

Later, I offered up some Kendal Mint Cake, which momentarily tricked us into thinking we had energy. We did not. But we plodded on, the rate of our movement now so slow it would've made a glacier look like a speedboat.

By the time we reached the Inversnaid Hotel waterfall, I'd gone from "a bit sore" to "one wrong step from full-blown Victorian invalid." It took me twenty minutes—*twenty*—to cover the last couple of hundred yards. That's not hiking. That's something you see in inspirational documentaries with piano music and captions about never giving up.

Robin and Chris were waiting at the top of the path by the falls. I limped up, defeated, and delivered the news: I was done. Finished. There was no bravado left. I suspected shin splints, which, for the uninitiated, is code for "you're walking like a drunk flamingo and it's not going to get better."

But I had a cunning plan.

I could still drive, I reckoned. If one of them went back to Milngavie to get the car, I could become our very own support vehicle—setting up camp, ferrying their bags, cheering from the sidelines like an overweight pit crew.

But no. Robin and Chris looked at each other, then delivered their verdict. "We've been watching your sad shuffle for the last two hours," they said, "and we've already decided—we're stopping here. If one of us can't finish, none of us will."

I nearly cried. Not just because it was touching, but also because my shin felt like it had been tasered.

Rob reminded me that he'd had to bow out of a walk the previous year after injuring himself getting out of the *car*, and we'd all bailed immediately. It made me feel slightly less like a failure. Slightly.

So, what next? We were, as usual, in the middle of nowhere. Through the trees, we could see the Inversnaid Hotel, so we figured we'd hobble there and see what our options were.

By the time I arrived (ten minutes after the others, obviously), another hiker had turned up. He was coming *back* from Fort William. I don't know what they put in the water up here, but these people think nothing of walking a hundred miles and then *turning around* to do it again. I was genuinely starting to feel like evolution had skipped me.

The hotel was closed. Not just locked— *abandoned*. The other hiker had spent half an hour knocking on every door. Pandemic closures, we reckoned. Too remote, too expensive to run, and too full of weary walkers asking for plasters.

He suggested a taxi, which would cost about the same as a second-hand hatchback, so I whipped out my trusty guidebook to see what other options we had. No train station. No buses. Just one potential escape route: the boat.

Cruise Loch Lomond, it said. Phone number included. Worth a shot.

I called, explained our sad little situation, and the lovely lady on the other end *laughed at me* for a full ten seconds before confirming a boat would come collect us shortly. Cheers, empathy.

As the boat chugged into view, I began the agonising limp down to the jetty. It took so long the boat had docked, turned around, made a cup of tea, and written its memoirs before I arrived. I limped the last few steps like a racewalker with one shoe nailed to the ground.

A young crewman offered me a hand aboard, probably so I didn't die in front of witnesses. Behind me, I heard peals of laughter from Robin and Chris, who, it turns out, had found their comedic moment of the day.

"You'll only have to pay half price," Rob said.

I looked blankly at him.

"They charge per leg," he grinned.

I hate him.

I hobbled across the deck, doing my best not to fall straight into the loch. I nearly succeeded. A set of steep steps led down into the cabin, and I threw my rucksack ahead of me like a sacrificial offering, helpful in case I tumbled after it.

Inside, the cabin was warm, surprisingly plush, and—most unexpectedly—had a bar. Yes, a *bar*. It was still early, and we were still technically in hiking mode, but my enthusiasm for rules had started to flag somewhere around the point where my leg stopped functioning like a leg.

The boat chugged northward up the loch. A pleasant voice began telling us about Rob Roy's

Cave, and it dawned on me that we were now on a *tourist boat*. The only other passengers were a young couple, who looked at us like we'd escaped from a boot camp for the criminally insane. Which, to be fair, wasn't entirely wrong.

The disembodied narrator turned out to be an actual person named Rory—cheerful, informative, and far too helpful for someone who had to deal with people like us. I asked about transport options, with a slight emphasis on the whole "my leg is currently held together by spite and ibuprofen" situation. Rory confirmed that yes, we *could* wave down a 70mph Citylink coach on the other side of the loch, but there was a far less suicidal option: a train from Tarbet. Lovely. Rory even told us the time, platform number, and price, which was frankly above and beyond. I would have hugged him, but I stank.

With time to kill, I suggested we pop outside to get some fresh air and a couple of photos. Rob wasn't moving. Probably frozen to the seat or morally opposed to breezes. Chris and I climbed back up the ladder to the top deck.

It was *Baltic*.

A wind cut across the loch with the kind of enthusiasm you normally only see in films about Arctic exploration. We managed one quick photo before being huffed off the deck by a rather large family who had all the warmth of a tax audit. When I say rather large, I don't mean in headcount.

I tried to apologise for merely existing as I squeezed back past them and descended the stairs. One of them followed behind—Dad, I presume— hovering so closely I thought he might try to overtake me on the steps. I briefly considered launching myself down all at once to get out of the way but chickened out and took it one at a time.

He was heading to the bar. Naturally. And for once, I felt the smug glow of moral superiority. At least until I sat down and discovered that someone —presumably Rob—had already bought me a coffee. A *very nice* coffee. Suspiciously nice. One sip told me exactly why.

There was a little something in it. A little something that would've made Rob Roy give a thumbs up from the grave.

So much for virtue. I drank it anyway.

Rory returned with actual printed train times, details of the transfer at Westerton (wherever that is), and the ticket price. I was halfway to asking him if he did piggybacks when I stopped myself. The man deserved a medal. We thanked him profusely and *definitely* didn't tell him we'd already Googled all that on the boat's Wi-Fi.

After an hour of bobbing around the loch like an injured rubber duck, we pulled into Tarbet. I waited for the healthy, able-bodied folk to disembark first—i.e., everyone else—then limped heroically across the deck and onto the dock, determined not to plunge into the icy waters of Loch Lomond as a final flourish.

Tarbet was lovely—a little place with big views and absolutely no concept of flat walking. I caught up to Robin and Chris and we headed toward what looked like a café on the map, which turned out to be a portakabin with dreams. Still, we had three hours until our train, and my stomach had filed a formal complaint.

I told them to go ahead and order for me, with the very generous intention of dodging the bill. They set off with confidence, immediately took the wrong turning, and then vanished into the distance like lost delivery drivers.

The walk wasn't far, but my leg had other ideas. Every step felt like a mistake. Houses lined the road, sturdy little things, probably built to survive winter gales, summer monsoons, and the occasional tourist breakdown. I remembered something someone once told me about Scottish weather: *"We have a word for when it's cold, grey, miserable and wet. We call it 'summer.'"* I chuckled. Then checked to make sure no one had seen me laughing to myself like a madman.

Up ahead, I spotted two figures in conversation with two more—one pair clearly Robin and Chris, the other in police uniforms. My first thought:

What have they done now? My second: *If we're arrested, I won't have to walk any further.*

As I hobbled closer, I realised the police weren't arresting them—they were speed trapping passing cars. Which, in fairness, is about as exciting as things get around here. Of course, Robin and Chris were bothering them. And of *course*, the officers had been told about me and my tragic limp.

"We clocked you at one mile an hour," the officer grinned, aiming his radar gun at me. Unless it was a taser. Frankly, I was open to either.

They explained the area was a known speeding hotspot, and we chatted briefly before letting them get back to annoying the locals. The portakabin café wasn't far off now, and when I caught up again, Robin proudly announced he'd already ordered sausage, bacon, and egg sandwiches for everyone.

A hero.

I sat down outside on a tiny bench and admired a sign that promised *"Free Toilets."* A rare and beautiful phrase. After three days of peeing behind trees, it felt like discovering El Dorado.

We all took full advantage. Then, inevitably, I set off for the train station well ahead of the others so they could catch me up by the time I got there. Which, of course, they did—just as I was wheezing up the steps to the single platform like a man climbing Everest in slippers.

Robin and Chris had already taken over the waiting room, spreading out their gear like feral commuters. Robin lit the stove and soon had coffee on the go. Bliss.

Then a man in a hi-vis jacket turned up and began "cleaning" the waiting room window with the intensity of someone who had been specifically told to keep an eye on us. He never said a word—just scrubbed and glared. Definitely clocked us as English.

Time passed. Our train wasn't due until just after 2pm, and the departure board showed nothing else. So we were genuinely thrilled when a long, mysterious freight train rumbled through. I was tempted to jump on it just to go somewhere —anywhere—but figured it would end with me slipping under the wheels and being diced into hiker confetti.

A short while later, a passenger train arrived. Totally unlisted. People got on and off like it was the most normal thing in the world. An elderly lady got off with a bicycle and confidently marched in the *wrong* direction down the platform, all the way to the far end, before realising her mistake and scuttling back past us, avoiding eye contact. Understandably.

We were still chuckling when the *actual* train arrived.

Boarding the train at Tarbet felt like being

rescued from a mountain by helicopter. I practically kissed the floor. It wasn't glamorous —just a standard ScotRail job—but I have never been so happy to sit in a slightly stained seat surrounded by strangers and damp Gore-Tex in my life.

I'd hobbled into the designated disabled spot, because—well—I *was*, at least temporarily, disabled. Robin and Chris sat opposite, with Robin immediately asked by a stranger if he needed the toilet. Strange. I began to suspect he just has a face that screams "I'm holding it in."

The train climbed gently, and we were treated to views that made me forget for a moment that my left leg was now essentially ornamental. We looked down on Loch Long, its name entirely accurate, and passed through all four seasons in half an hour—sunshine, wind, snow, and a light dusting of Scottish passive-aggression.

Eventually, we hit Dalmuir. This was where we had to buy tickets for the journey we'd *already taken*—a bureaucratic exercise in time travel. I hobbled into the ticket office and explained to the young man behind the desk that we'd come from Tarbet and needed tickets to Milngavie.

"Have you forgotten something in Tarbet?" he asked earnestly.

"No," I replied, "I've forgotten how to use my legs. I'd just like a ticket to Milngavie."

He blinked at me, clearly trying to figure out what kind of scam this was. I repeated myself. Eventually, with all the enthusiasm of a man being forced to do algebra in a canoe, he printed three tickets and charged us less than a tenner, when it should have been three times that.

I emerged from the ticket office stunned. The man behind me, who'd been on our train and heard the whole thing, realised he could do the same and now looked like he'd just won the lottery in five-pence pieces.

After a quick change at Westerton (which, let's be honest, might as well be Narnia for all anyone knows), we were on the final train to Milngavie. It was packed. Pandemic, remote Scottish village, Tuesday afternoon... and the train looked like the Tube at rush hour.

We stayed put until the chaos passed, not wanting to take out innocent civilians with our giant rucksacks and damp odour. An unconscious man at the back was being heckled by school kids, until he let out an ungodly fart, yawned, and woke up mid-drowse like a bear emerging from hibernation. That shut them up.

Milngavie station was *huge* by comparison— multiple platforms, a shop, toilets, baby changing facilities (in case you want to exchange your baby for a better one), and—most importantly—a car park.

I collapsed onto the first bit of concrete I saw and instructed Robin and Chris to go fetch the car. On the train, we'd debated whether to drive home or stop somewhere en route. But then Rob came up with an idea so good I was furious I hadn't thought of it: we'd ring Frances at Kip in the Kirk and see if she could take us in again.

She could.

Then we rang the Clachan Inn, Scotland's oldest pub (by its own self-important declaration), and they had space at 6.45pm. The stars had aligned.

Naturally, when the lads returned with the car, I told them Frances was full and we'd have to sleep in a ditch. Their faces fell. It was glorious. Then I revealed the truth, and they nearly wept with joy.

Rob drove like a man late for his own wedding, and we handbrake-turned into the Kirk driveway. I limped inside like I'd just crossed the Alps. The kettle was on. The scones were still warm. Frances, once again, was a national treasure.

She mentioned another guest called Nicholas was floating about somewhere, and then disappeared off to give someone a driving lesson, her day job, apparently. Trusting soul.

Three hot showers later, we were pub-ready. I set off for the Clachan two days before the others to ensure we arrived together—because the one rule of pub dining is never be the first one there. That way, you never have to buy the first round. Not that it mattered—booze was still banned in pubs at this point in the pandemic, because obviously alcohol is what makes COVID contagious after 6pm.

When we arrived, Robin tried to check in for our table. No dice. He ran through every possible name: Rob, Robin, Chris, Paul, even our surnames (which I won't repeat, in case you *are* the axe murderer).

Eventually, I stepped forward and whispered, "Try the name *Attrick. Gerry Attrick*."

It worked. Obviously.

We sat down, masks off—because apparently, the virus can't see you when you're seated—and studied the menu. I went for curry. Chris picked a pie the size of a football. Robin chose something involving chicken. Naturally, mine was the worst of the three.

Chris ate his pie like a man slowly unwrapping a Christmas gift just to make me suffer.

There would be no celebratory pint to wash it down. COVID rules. Instead, we walked to the shop and *accidentally* bought a few beers to drink back at the Kirk. For hydration. Obviously.

Back at base, a well-spoken stranger was drinking our tea and eating our scones. This, we deduced, was Nicholas.

He spoke like someone who thought *Waitrose*

was a bit rough. Very polite, very posh, and prone to "pardon?" every time we opened our mouths. He was doing the route with a baggage courier (something I would 100% do if I weren't so cheap) and had, curiously, skipped Day One by taking the train from Milngavie. We said nothing. Each to their own. He seemed the type who would disappear in a puff of pipe smoke at any moment.

We offered him a beer. He declined. Said he was getting up early. Probably to levitate his way up Ben Lomond before breakfast.

Robin and Chris entertained him with tales of injury, mishaps, and What3Words—a magical app for lost fools. Nick downloaded it instantly. I helpfully suggested it could be used to call mountain rescue *or* to find your wife in the Waitrose car park. He didn't laugh. Probably because he shops at Fortnum & Mason.

That night, as we sat in the lounge sipping beer and trading mockery, it finally sank in. This was it. *The end of the road—for now.* My leg was swollen like a balloon animal, and even the hobble to the pub had been a victory of grit over common sense.

The next day, after finally making it home and shuffling into A&E, the diagnosis came in: anterior shin splint. Rest. Ice. Elevation. And, most importantly, *milk it for all it's worth*, which I fully intended to do. My wife was thrilled, obviously.

The West Highland Way wasn't finished. But it

wasn't going anywhere. We'd be back. Eventually.
Unless it killed me first.

Inversnaid To Crianlarich

What happens in the tent stays in the tent.

Unknown

Several months had passed since I'd hobbled off the West Highland Way like a man auditioning for a role as "Injured Extra Number 3" in *Braveheart*. After some doctorly prodding and a few physio sessions that involved more wincing than walking, I finally felt ready to finish what we'd started back in May.

To test the waters (and the legs), Rob, Chris and I had squeezed in a few shorter walks over the summer. I'd also invested in a pair of compression socks—supposedly the magic cure for shin splints, though frankly they felt more like sausage casings designed for human legs. Still, they came highly recommended by the internet, and what could *that* possibly get wrong?

The summer itself had been a revolving door of lockdowns, restrictions, and confusing tier systems that even the government didn't understand. But we'd managed to keep vaguely fit, despite our increasingly middle-aged commitments and the fact that beer exists.

And so, by the end of August—specifically the bank holiday week—we were back on the road, northbound once again, heading into the land of kilts, haggis, Buckfast and the airborne embodiment of Scottish vengeance: the midge.

We'd been in touch with Frances from Kip in the Kirk in Drymen, who graciously agreed to let us use her cottage next to the Clachan Inn as our base for the week. It's usually a B&B, but we rented it self-catering, mainly so our families could stay in comfort while the three of us trudged off to play at being Bear Grylls with blisters.

The plan was simple. Drive up on Sunday, eat something greasy, and catch the ferry from Tarbet to Inversnaid first thing Monday morning. From there, we'd rejoin the trail, finish the job, and maybe come out the other side a little fitter or at least slightly less broken.

Any doubts I'd once had about splitting the walk were long gone. In fact, we were now looking forward to the next stretch with actual enthusiasm—mostly because we suspected the most spectacular parts of the Highlands were still to come. And, miraculously, the weather forecast agreed. Sunshine. All week. Glorious. Possibly a lie, but we were choosing hope over experience for once.

Of course, with late August sunshine in Scotland comes the inevitable tax: the midge. I'd taken to checking the midge forecast daily, which, yes, is a real thing. Once I got over the sheer *existence* of a midge forecast, I was dismayed to see it wasn't exactly promising.

The forecast works on a scale from zero to five —zero meaning the midges are all on holiday, five meaning the air is essentially soup made of flying teeth. Drymen was sitting at a manageable 'two.' Fort William, on the other hand—our grand finale —was clocking in at a full-blown 'five.' A level-five midge situation is not to be taken lightly. It's like being mugged by the atmosphere.

Oddly enough, Sunday night passed without much insect drama. Then again, we barely stepped outside, preferring the safety of walls, windows and a decent roof. Our only excursion was a pilgrimage to Balloch in search of a Chinese takeaway, which ended in success at The Princess Rose.

Disappointingly, not one of the town's Chinese takeaways had been named *Wok Lomond*, which I thought was a criminally wasted pun and a solid business opportunity, should anyone fancy franchising.

Back at the cottage, I tried to light some incense to ward off any rogue midges that might have followed us back. The resulting inferno triggered the smoke alarm and earned me a fresh round of marital judgement. Apparently, they weren't incense sticks, they were *fragrance sticks*, and not meant to be set on fire. Who knew? I still argue that the smoke worked. At the very least, it stunned the midges into silence and possibly scorched a few.

The lack of winged tormentors lulled us into a false sense of security. I suspected we'd pay for it later. But at that moment, belly full of sweet and sour chicken and sinuses full of eau de smouldering fragrance stick, I drifted off to sleep, quietly optimistic and entirely unprepared for what the trail had in store next.

I couldn't decide whether the promised sunshine would make the midge situation better or worse. Would it fry them? Or simply encourage them to reproduce faster, like little airborne gremlins? Either way, we'd find out soon enough— because tomorrow we were heading out to see for ourselves. This thrilling realisation filled me with the sort of nervous anticipation usually reserved for dental work and Ryanair flights.

I barely slept. It was just like the night before a school trip, except instead of clutching a Walkman and some Panda Pops, I lay awake stressing about blisters, compression socks and whether Rob had packed enough rum. Eventually, I must have dozed off, because when I opened my eyes, it was morning and the room was bathed in that particular shade of grey that says, "Don't bother with sunglasses."

Dragging myself out of bed felt like abandoning a trusted friend. I already knew I'd miss this mattress more than most people. Ahead of us lay wild camping—no more bothies, no more cosy B&Bs, and absolutely no chance of finding anything remotely as lovely as Kip in the Kirk. Just tents, stoves, and Scottish weather. Glorious.

I pulled back the curtains to find the sky looking like a particularly depressed sponge. Overcast. Damp. That sort of weather that doesn't quite rain but somehow still makes you wet. The BBC had promised sun, but I suspected their meteorologist was either blind, on drugs, or an optimist—which, frankly, is worse.

We had one final breakfast with the ladies, our last civilised meal before the reintroduction of dehydrated slop and eating while crouched behind a rock. Post-eggs, we went through the age-old ritual of hiker foot maintenance, lovingly plastering every toe, heel and hotspot with preventative Compeed in a desperate bid to avoid foot-based carnage by lunchtime.

Rob and Chris were thoroughly entertained by my ongoing battle with the compression socks. These things came up to my knees and required the strength and flexibility of a Cirque du Soleil performer to actually get on. It was less "getting dressed" and more "birthing a new leg." I hoped they'd help with the shin splints— and the recurring issue of my left ankle behaving like it had been borrowed from someone less structurally sound.

Eventually, after much straining, stretching, and a fair bit of wheezing, we were ready to go. We lobbed our bags into Rob's car and hit the road towards Tarbet. The journey was peaceful, scenic and—oh joy—punctuated by the squeak of windscreen wipers. Of course it was raining. Of course it was. I glared at the sky and made peace with the fact that, in Scotland, the weather forecast is less a prediction and more a polite suggestion.

We cruised around the southern edge of Loch Lomond, through the charming town of Balloch, and half an hour later rolled into Tarbet. This was where I'd last dragged myself off the trail months earlier, limping like an injured gazelle with a shopping bag full of rocks. Today, though, I walked across the car park like a man reborn. Or at least, like a man who hadn't torn anything important *yet*.

While we popped over to chat with the boat operator, the women wisely stayed in the car to avoid the rain. They were joining us for the boat trip across the loch, doing a nice round tour while we got off at Inversnaid to resume our slow trudge northward into pain and puddles.

I nudged my son Max and told him to keep an eye out for wallabies. He gave me the look. The one that says, *you've lied to me before, old man*. Fair.

"I'm not kidding this time," I said, although admittedly the odds of seeing one today were slim to none. The wallabies live on Inchconnachan Island, which is both impossible to spell and entirely invisible from here.

But the wallabies are real. They were introduced by Fiona Bryde Colquhoun, the Countess of Arran —an eccentric aristocrat who combined animal rights activism with a passion for competitive powerboating. As you do. She was known as "the fastest granny on water," which is the sort of title you'd expect to find in a steamy romance novel rather than the Guinness Book of Records.

She brought wallabies, llamas, pigs—you name it—to the island so they could live happily ever after, which they've been doing for the last 80 years. Until now. Because modern conservationists, with their clipboards and frowns, want the wallabies *removed*. Apparently, they pose a threat to the native capercaillie, a rare Scottish bird best described as "a black grouse with delusions of grandeur."

Personally, I feel that if the wallabies haven't wiped them out in the last eight decades, they're probably not that much of a threat. And if they *have* wiped them out, then it's a bit late to start getting cross now. Either way, I vote wallabies.

Back on the pier, the boat captain informed us he'd be departing at 10:30 sharp and that boarding would start ten minutes prior. He also confirmed that the rain was "set in"—which is local speak for "this is your life now." We retreated to the car to sulk in dry, vaguely heated silence.

Not a single sunbeam pierced the clouds. Not even a teasing flicker. I cursed the BBC and remembered that this was the same organisation whose proudest forecasting moment involved Michael Fish telling the nation not to worry about a hurricane—mere hours before Britain was flattened in the Great Storm of 1987. Nineteen people died, 15 million trees fell over, and Sevenoaks briefly became Oneoak. So no, I wasn't putting my faith in their sunny optimism.

Still, as I always say: a bit of rain never killed anyone. Unless it was the torrential kind. With lightning. And a dodgy river crossing. But still—generally speaking.

Ten minutes before the boat left, we ambled down to the pier. I took the opportunity to walk with my wife, hand in hand, soaking up a last bit of affection before disappearing into the hills. Chris, seeing this, couldn't help himself. "How've you been married so long and still hold hands?" he asked.

I smiled. "Because if I let go, she'll wander off

and buy something."

Finally boarding the boat, we were joined by a cast of characters that felt less like fellow travellers and more like extras from a low-budget travel documentary. First up was a young man with a fly-fishing obsession and a name to match—Bernard. Yes, *Bernard*. He told us about his angling plans with all the fervour of a man who regularly argues with trout.

He proudly showed off his homemade flies—which, yes, that *is* apparently the correct term. What he'd created, though, looked less like traditional fishing gear and more like the contents of a Victorian haunted dollhouse. Gargoyles, grotesques, vaguely insectoid nightmares, all lovingly handcrafted to tempt fish with no discernible standards. Still, Bernard seemed pleased. The fish, less so, probably.

Also on board: a rather mature couple who immediately settled in at the front of the boat and proceeded to canoodle their way across the loch, utterly indifferent to the dramatic scenery outside. Loch Lomond? Waterfalls? Misty peaks? No thanks, we'll just fondle each other's faces for forty minutes, cheers.

Then there was an elderly lady with a bicycle. She spent the entire journey nervously circling the life rafts and making absolutely sure her bike didn't fall overboard. Or possibly making sure *she* didn't have to use the bike as a flotation device. Either way, she seemed suspiciously prepared for a nautical disaster.

I sat and talked with my wife for a while and made an honest attempt at sentimentality, telling her I'd miss her this week. The look she gave me suggested she thought I had a secret agenda, which is ridiculous—I'd *already* packed the snacks. I even told her, quite sincerely, that if the boat sank and there was only one life jacket between us, I'd miss her dearly and think of her every single day. She was unmoved.

Max and I ventured briefly to the upper deck for a better view. We lasted roughly a minute before deciding that yes, visibility was rubbish and no, we didn't want to die of exposure before lunchtime. Down we went again, back to the warmish cabin and the company of Bernard's bug collection.

The views, despite the fog, still had a rugged charm. We could see the loch and the treeline, but anything above that had been swallowed by the clouds. It was like sailing through the inside of a teabag.

No one else was out on the water, and given the conditions, that wasn't surprising. The rain was persistent, the air was soggy, and our collective enthusiasm was beginning to smell faintly of damp Gore-Tex. Rob, Chris and I discussed the likelihood of getting soaked. Again. Just like we did on the very first leg from Milngavie to Drymen. A nostalgic full-circle moment, if you like your circles damp and itchy.

By the time the boat reached Inversnaid, we were dressed like waterproof onions. Every layer we owned was on. And yes, I was wearing my hat. The same hat the others mocked. The same hat that keeps both rain and sun at bay. They still didn't bring one. Fools.

We disembarked last, following Bernard and the lady-with-the-bike, and I made an Olympic-level leap over the unnecessarily large gap between boat and dock, determined not to start the day with a plunge into Loch Lomond.

At the top of the dock was a bench—clearly placed for dramatic goodbyes. We dropped our rucksacks and gave one final wave to the womenfolk and Max, who were now heading off to learn about caves and hydroelectric infrastructure in relative comfort.

This was the moment Rob chose to wind up his wife by pretending he'd forgotten to hand over the car keys. Her face froze for half a second in sheer panic before she realised he was winding her up and rightfully called him an idiot. A fair and accurate assessment.

As the boat vanished into the fog like some romantic metaphor for our sanity, we found ourselves alone on the dock—three men, some backpacks, and an overwhelming sense of déjà vu. Same place, same time of day, just several months (and a few injuries) later. This was it. The reunion tour. The sequel. *West Highland Way 2: Soggy Reckoning.*

We shouldered our bags and headed off. Mine, I'm happy to report, was noticeably lighter than last time. Turns out, backpacking isn't about what you bring—it's about what you learn *not* to bring. I'd ditched enough unnecessary junk to open a small outdoor shop, and my shin was deeply grateful.

But our triumphant return lasted all of fifty feet. Because standing just ahead of us was Glenn.

Glenn was a ranger with the Loch Lomond and the Trossachs National Park Service, which is possibly the longest job title in existence that still doesn't explain what you actually do. Rob asked him about the weather. Glenn looked up, blinked at the sky, and said, with admirable professionalism, "It's raining."

He then grinned and explained it was a local pattern and that we'd walk out of it soon enough. This was either comforting or a masterclass in vague optimism. I asked how lockdown and COVID had affected the park, expecting tales of eerie silence and serene woodlands. Instead, he told us it had been *busier* than ever, mostly thanks to irresponsible campers and wildlife crime.

Now, when someone says "wildlife crime," most people might think of poaching or illegal hunting. Not me. My brain immediately conjured up visions of delinquent squirrels mugging picnickers or feral goats running black-market nut rings. I laughed out loud. No one else did. There was a brief silence where even Glenn seemed to reassess his life choices.

He reminded us to check out the waterfall next to the hotel (which we already had), and then said there wasn't much else to see here. Bold claim, considering the view across Loch Lomond is one of the finest in the country. But maybe he was just being modest. Or possibly blind.

Before we moved on, he told us a brilliantly pointless fact: Inversnaid used to have a school. A very expensive one. Because it only had *two* pupils. And those two pupils were the children of the headmaster, who had moved there specifically to run the school. So he brought his family with him to teach them, in a building that could've served a small town. Government efficiency at its finest.

With that, we said goodbye to Glenn and hit the trail properly. A nearby signpost pointed us north and we started off along a narrow, twisty path that clung to the shoreline like it owed it money. The ground was a mess of rocks and exposed tree roots, all of which were clearly trying to trip us and hurl us into the loch.

Just a few hundred yards in, I saw the perfect campsite by a boathouse. Right on the water. Flat, sheltered, beautiful. Naturally, we didn't need it *now*, which is exactly when you always find these places. I stared at it longingly, filed it away under *Missed Opportunities*, and pressed on.

Rob and Chris were off again, powering ahead with all the enthusiasm of spaniels chasing a stick, while I—firmly at the back—trundled along at the speed of a thoughtful sloth. They stopped once or twice after just a few hundred feet, presumably to check I hadn't collapsed or been eaten by a bear, but I waved them on.

"No need to wait," I told them. "I'll catch you up eventually." Which I would. Eventually. I explained that I wasn't about to rush just to end up broken again. I'd learned my lesson: if you go at someone else's pace, you inherit their injuries. I was sticking to my own rhythm. That rhythm just happened to be half a mile an hour slower than theirs, which over time translates into being about three villages behind.

Walking solo gave me a rare opportunity to reflect on life, the landscape, and the fact that I was currently shuffling down a slippy boulder on my backside like a pensioner on a playground slide. Midway through this elegant descent, I heard a sound no hiker ever wants to hear—a distinct *rrrip*.

Panic.

I froze. Had something torn? Had I just mooned Loch Lomond? A quick check revealed nothing immediately catastrophic, but the seed of doubt had been planted. I made a mental note to inspect things more closely later—and maybe not bend down until then. I hadn't packed spare trousers, only spare pants. Priorities.

Thankfully, the ladies were meeting us the next day at Bridge of Orchy with fresh supplies—pants, snacks, and, crucially, rum. The holy trinity of any Scottish hike.

I carried on, now moving with a little more caution and a lot more paranoia. As I rounded a bend, I caught a horrific smell that stopped me dead in my tracks. For a moment, I wondered if Rob was having some kind of gastric emergency. It wouldn't be his first. But no—this wasn't your average post-bacon-roll flatulence. This was something *otherworldly*.

I emerged onto the path to find the true culprits: two wild goats, standing in the middle of the trail like they owned it. They stared at me. I stared back. They bleated. I considered retreating. They didn't move an inch—probably because they were waiting to see if I'd keel over from the stench.

It was honestly the worst thing I've smelt since I worked at a warehouse that imported legal drugs from North America. And yes, I do mean *legal* drugs. Nothing suspicious—just pallets of medicinal lotions and tablets. Mostly.

Except for one memorable shipment, which contained a surprise passenger: a raccoon. A *very dead* raccoon. Judging by the state of it, it hadn't survived the Atlantic crossing, or possibly even the first half hour of packing. The smell was... well, let's just say it stuck with me. Literally. We abandoned the pallet, called the manager, and decided he could deal with it—because frankly, if you earn the big bucks, you can wrestle with the wildlife corpses.

Back to the goats. These weren't your average farmyard types. These were ancient, feral beasts —possibly immortal, definitely unbothered. The ones you'll meet along this stretch of the trail are thought to have been released after the First World War by a nearby army base at Loch Ard, just a few miles east. Because obviously what every recovering woodland needs after a global conflict is a herd of farting horned vandals.

That said, goats have been a part of the Highlands for centuries. Inversnaid's scraggly lot, in particular, are among the oldest known, allegedly recorded as far back as the 12th century. Some even link them to Robert the Bruce himself. Legend has it he ordered goats to be slaughtered so that his newly planted yew trees—intended for longbow production—could grow in peace. Which is all very noble and strategic, but also quite rude if you happen to be a goat.

There's some doubt about this version of events, though. Mainly because yew trees take roughly the entire reign of the Plantagenets to grow a single usable branch. So either Robert the Bruce was planning *very* far ahead or someone embellished the story after a few too many ales.

Later, from around 1700 to 1920, the whole area was heavily forested—commercially, this time—and goats were definitely not welcome, what with their tendency to eat everything, including the concept of forest sustainability. So odds are the goats we see today aren't directly descended from Bruce's era. Which is a shame, because that would've made them historic. Now they're just... smelly.

Still, I like to imagine that at least a *bit* of ancient DNA has survived. Modern feral goats *look* ancient, but that's mostly because domestic animals left to go rogue quickly revert to a kind of wild default setting. Same with pigs. The process even has a name: epigenetics. It's when genes behave differently depending on their environment, turning your average goat into something you'd expect to see drawn on a cave wall by a terrified caveman.

This led me, as most things do, to a worrying thought: what would *we* look like after a week in the wild? With no showers, limited hygiene, and diets consisting mostly of trail mix and regret, I suspected the transformation might already be underway.

I shuddered and kept walking. The goats stared after me, possibly out of curiosity, possibly because they were plotting.

About a mile further up the loch, a sign pointed us left, down a narrow side trail promising something we'd been looking forward to: Rob Roy's Cave. At last, a bit of history to break up the endless tripping hazard that is this part of the West Highland Way.

We dropped our packs by the main path and left them there with the usual naïve faith in humanity that assumes someone won't immediately walk off with them. The cave wasn't far—just a short, steep detour almost to the loch shore. Definitely worth a visit. Absolutely *not* worth lugging a 15-kilo backpack down to.

We'd actually spotted the cave from the boat the last time we passed through Inversnaid, but only because someone had helpfully daubed the word *CAVE* on the rocks in massive white letters. Subtlety clearly not a priority for the local historical society.

It took a bit of effort to get inside. There was a narrow crack in the rocks, which required some gentle manoeuvring and for Rob, a full-body exorcism. Once we squeezed in, we found the cave's current residents: an enthusiastic colony of spiders, several of which had brought their babies along. Hundreds of them. Swinging from silk hammocks like tiny eight-legged psychopaths. Lovely.

Rob Roy himself is said to have used this cave as a hideout during his cattle-rustling days—which, let's be honest, was pretty much his entire CV. As hideouts go, it was hardly a Bond villain's lair. More a damp cupboard with a body count. I couldn't picture him spending any real length of time in there unless he had a thing for close quarters and arachnids. But perhaps that was the genius of it—no one else would willingly follow him in.

After a few minutes of breathing through our mouths and pretending not to panic, we crawled back out into daylight and rejoined our bags, which, miraculously, had not been nicked. Back on the trail, we resumed our merry shuffle along the endless, squelchy edge of Loch Lomond.

I was glad we'd made the detour, especially since we'd missed Rob Roy's *Prison*—another cave, apparently, which lies further south between Rowardennan and Inversnaid. The story goes that Roy once kidnapped the Sheriff of Dumbartonshire and held him there for a week. Probably ransom. Possibly boredom. Either way, we'd walked straight past it without realising, proving once again that our navigational skills were somewhere between 'random' and 'legally actionable.'

The forest in this stretch was gorgeously moody —gnarled trees, lush ferns, and the sort of persistent drizzle that says *"Welcome to Scotland. Here's a reminder you're not waterproof."* It felt ancient, as if the whole place had been preserved in bracken and moss. Which it probably had.

We continued through a landscape best described as a 3D obstacle course: clambering over slick rocks, dodging roots that acted more like tentacles, and dealing with inclines that clearly hadn't been consulted about accessibility.

The weather, in case you were wondering, had *not* improved. In fact, it had leaned into the whole "biblical" vibe and cranked things up a notch. Thankfully, the tree cover kept us from becoming completely saturated. Just moderately soggy and lightly irritable. It was all very reminiscent of our Day One trudge to Drymen, a memory I had carefully repressed until that very moment.

Around a particularly sharp bend, we caught up with an elderly couple who were clearly struggling with the terrain. Navigating this stretch of trail is hard enough with knees that haven't seen a warranty in over a decade, and these two looked like they were auditioning for a Werther's Original advert.

Rob, playing the role of Gentle Giant, immediately offered to help. He grabbed the woman's rucksack and passed it to me while he went back for her hand. At which point he slipped, almost did a reverse swan dive into the loch, and had to be steadied by the very woman he was trying to assist. Which raised the question—who exactly was helping who?

Still, we got them through the rocky bit in one piece and stopped to chat. Turns out they were veterans of several long-distance walks, including Hadrian's Wall and the coast-to-coast route, and were wondering if perhaps their hiking days were numbered. "This section is *relentless,*" they said, with the haunted eyes of people who'd just done a few accidental squats too many.

The man told me he was seventy. "You don't look a day over sixty-nine," I replied, delivering the same joke I'd now used approximately seventeen times since beginning this trip. He laughed anyway, which I appreciated. Or maybe he was just relieved to be alive.

They were a charming pair. The lady proudly listed the Pennine Way, Thames Path, and South Downs Way among their conquests, while her husband leaned in and whispered, "Ignore my wife. She tends to ramble." Wordplay. From a pensioner. Peak comedy.

I wished them luck and jog-shuffled off to catch up with Rob and Chris, who were somewhere ahead, no doubt arguing over whose turn it was to carry the emergency pork pies.

It wasn't long before Rob and Chris disappeared up the path again, galloping into the mist like a pair of over-eager trail ponies. I followed at my own carefully curated pace—a speed best described as "measured," or possibly "barely moving but upright."

A few twists and turns later, I caught up with them again. Or at least, I caught up with Rob's rucksack... because he'd taken it off and was now wedged between a tree and a rock in what can only be described as a very intimate encounter with nature.

Ahead of us, the trail narrowed into one of those natural bottlenecks that feels specifically designed to humiliate anyone over a size medium. A large slab of rock sat smugly against a particularly inconsiderate tree, forming a gap just wide enough for a thinly sliced teenager. For anyone else— particularly for Rob, who as we've previously established is a "big unit"—this was a challenge bordering on architectural insult.

Rob had already taken his backpack off and was attempting to wedge himself through sideways, grunting with the kind of determination usually reserved for child birth or trying to cancel a broadband contract. Eventually, through a combination of willpower and soft tissue compression, he made it.

Chris then strolled through like he was gliding

into a revolving door at John Lewis. I followed with a bit more huff and puff, but managed it without incident. Rob, now free but clearly traumatised, stormed on ahead in a sulk, knowing full well that the jokes were incoming and unstoppable.

We let him go in front—not because we trusted his navigation (we absolutely didn't), but because it gave us a much better view of his slightly dented pride.

The trail continued as a lochside dance of roots, rocks, and sudden drops, winding through trees that appeared to be plotting against us. Every corner revealed a new obstacle, every step a potential pratfall. Somewhere to our left, just out of reach across the shimmering loch, was a small wooded island—Island I Vow.

Now, if that sounds romantic, just wait.

This little island hides the ruins of a medieval castle, which was once the seat of Clan MacFarlane —famous for two things: being absolute masters of cattle theft and having the sort of nocturnal reputation that even rabid badgers would find excessive.

In fact, the full moon was known locally as *MacFarlane's Lantern* because that's when they did most of their thieving. They'd sneak out under the moonlight, pinch anything with four legs and a confused expression, then melt back into the woods before you'd finished your porridge.

Eventually, the government got fed up with all this moonlit mischief. In 1594, several senior MacFarlanes were dragged into court on charges of robbery, murder, and tyranny—a kind of criminal hat-trick. Some fled to Ireland, others to America, where they rebranded slightly and became the Macfarlands. A bit of a PR glow-up.

Interestingly, the position of Clan Chief is currently vacant. So if your surname is MacFarlane, Macfarland or something vaguely similar and you've got a decent beard and a fondness for tartan, you could technically apply for the role. Add that to your LinkedIn.

As the island faded from view, the trees around us began to thin out slightly. The oppressive forest opened into a series of mossy meadows, and just like that, the rain stopped. Not completely, but enough to make us believe that the BBC weather team weren't entirely made up of coffee-fuelled fantasists.

To our right, we got our first proper view of Ben Lomond—Scotland's southernmost Munro and the tallest thing we'd seen in hours that wasn't a tree or Rob in full rain gear. The clouds still clung stubbornly to its peak, like a hat that didn't quite fit, but it was nice to finally orient ourselves. It meant progress. Sort of.

The trail began to level out a bit. No more goat-inspired gymnastics. No more squeezing through rock/tree booby traps. Just nice, sensible hiking. And then we found it.

A pair of buildings emerged just off the trail —one charmingly derelict, the other surprisingly well-maintained. This was Doune Bothy, and had we not already agreed to walk on to Crianlarich, we might've been tempted to stop.

It wasn't quite as big as Rowchoish Bothy, but it looked just as cosy. Stone walls, a solid roof, and the kind of interior that says, "Yes, I am past my best, but what other choice do you have?"

Sure enough, inside we found half a dozen hikers and one Labrador—all friendly, all damp, and all ready to exchange the usual information: where you're going, where you've come from, and what colour your socks are. (OK, maybe not the last one, but it wouldn't have surprised me.)

One bloke told me that the ruin next door used to be owned by a member of U2. I asked which one. He said he wasn't sure.

We reluctantly tore ourselves away from the warm glow of the bothy—and, more heartbreakingly, from the Labrador—though not before hearing a few of the campers giggling as we left. Whether that was in appreciation of our general ruggedness or because one of us had something embarrassing stuck to their rucksack, I'll never know. I didn't have the courage to check my rear.

With only a couple of miles to go before our first proper stop of the day, spirits were high. That stop? The infamous Drovers Inn at Inverarnan —a pub older than the United States, perched just beyond the top of Loch Lomond on the River Falloch, and allegedly stuffed to the rafters with ghosts, whisky, and deeply questionable taxidermy. All the good stuff.

The trail to get there passed through a beautiful forest of hazel and oak, the sort of place woodland fairies would retire to if they'd had enough of glitter and joined the National Trust. The oaks were positively dripping with moss, in that dramatic Celtic rainforest style, which is a polite way of saying "it's very wet here, all the time, bring a coat."

Had I been any good at photography, I'm sure I could have captured some stunning scenes. Unfortunately, my camera skills tend to result in blurry tree trunks and a thumb in the corner, so you'll just have to take my word for it—it was stunning.

At one point, Rob pointed out something red and bulbous poking out of the undergrowth.

"Either that's a very confident toadstool," he said, "or I'm hallucinating."

Turned out it was a fly agaric mushroom—the one that looks like it's been copied and pasted straight out of a children's fairy tale or the loading screen of a Nintendo game. Big, red, white spots, unapologetically theatrical. Basically the Elton John of fungi.

Now, I'm not much of a mycologist (yes, that's the actual word for mushroom boffins), but even I knew this one: do *not* eat it. I shouldn't have to say that, but in today's world, there's always one person who thinks a foraged snack sounds like a good idea. It's not. This particular mushroom is famous for being both magical and mildly homicidal.

The Victorians, in all their baffling wisdom, loved putting pictures of these things on Christmas cards. Some even reckon it's the reason Santa wears red and white. And honestly, after walking through a rain-drenched forest while pondering psychedelic mushrooms, I can see how a man in a flying sleigh might've seemed perfectly plausible.

The fly agaric has a weird symbiotic relationship with birch trees, where it apparently shares nutrients with them. Lovely. However, if you eat one, you might find yourself chatting with squirrels or attempting to crawl into your own backpack. It's also thought to have inspired Alice in Wonderland's rabbit hole antics. Frankly, after five minutes staring at it, I started to feel dizzy myself. Time to move on.

Its name, if you're curious, comes from the fact

that it's deadly to flies. And possibly—hopefully—midges, which were beginning to swirl in the trees around us like they were rehearsing a coordinated attack.

The rest of the route toward the pub was fairly uneventful. Which, given the terrain so far, was a welcome change. No more goat ambushes. No rock-hugging contortion challenges. Just muddy paths and the occasional tree root with malicious intent.

Eventually, we crested a small hill and got our first glimpse of Beinglas Farm Campsite—and with it, civilisation. Sort of. Two women passed us on the trail and cheerfully told us we were only fifteen minutes from the Drovers Inn. Then they walked off, giggling.

I immediately assumed the worst. Was my fly down? Did I have a mushroom stuck to my backside? A quick inventory of zips and dignity revealed no obvious problems, so I chalked it up to paranoia and pressed on.

Forty-five minutes later—after trudging through mud, second-guessing directions, and questioning everything we thought we knew about time—we finally arrived.

The Drovers Inn.

Scotland's most haunted pub, and frankly, even if it had been entirely full of banshees playing bagpipes, we still would've gone in.

The building itself is a proper beauty—stone-built, weather-worn, and very much giving off "we've survived several rebellions and at least one demonic possession" energy. As we approached, it basically *beckoned* us inside with the promise of heat, ale, and possibly the ghost of a Jacobite or two.

True to our commitment to supporting the local economy (especially when it involves alcohol), we wandered in. And were promptly greeted by... a bear.

A stuffed one, obviously. At least, we *think* it was stuffed. It stood proudly by the entrance like a bouncer for a nature-themed nightclub. Naturally, Chris and I took turns sticking our hands in its mouth for a photo—because if you can't have a play, why bother hiking?

Rucksacks dumped at the door, we let Rob race to the bar, loudly insisting it was his round. None of us were arguing.

The inside was exactly what you want from an ancient Highland pub: heavy wooden beams, flickering lighting, and so much taxidermy it felt like a Victorian natural history museum had exploded. There were swords on the walls, stuffed animals on shelves, and the faint scent of wood smoke and ghost stories in the air.

If Hogwarts had a pub, it would look like this—only with slightly fewer angry spirits and probably worse whisky.

The Drovers Inn isn't just old—it's *haunted*. Which, to be fair, is par for the course in Scotland, where every third building either has a ghost, a tragic backstory, or both. If you're feeling especially brave (or just incredibly cheap and think "ghosts" are a good excuse for discounted accommodation), you can even stay overnight in one of their spookier rooms. For maximum fear and minimum sleep, they recommend room two or room six.

Room two allegedly plays host to the ghost of a little girl. Now, let's be honest here—there is *nothing* more terrifying than a ghost child. You can keep your howling banshees and headless horsemen. A silent child staring at you in the dead of night with hair like she's been dragged backwards through a hedge and eyes that say "I see your soul"... nope. Not for me, thanks.

And I speak from experience.

A few years back, I got up in the night for one of those half-asleep shuffles to the bathroom. I turned the corner onto the landing and froze. There, standing silently in the dark, was a small girl. Not moving. Not blinking. Just *standing*. Like a possessed Victorian doll left in the wrong century.

Now, allow me to clarify something important: I don't have a daughter. Just sons. And this thing? Not one of them.

As I stood there, wide-eyed and suddenly very aware of my own mortality, my brain scrambled to come up with some logical explanation—any explanation that didn't end in *"...and then they found me rocking in a cupboard, muttering about hair."* It eventually clicked that this was my niece, who'd come to stay and was, for reasons known only to Satan, sleepwalking. Either that or she was actively auditioning for *The Ring*.

Anyway, back to the Drovers Inn, where we were now happily settled into the much safer part of the pub—the one with the alcohol. We'd been propping up the bar for a while, chatting with the barman, who turned out to be a walking encyclopedia of whisky and ghost stories. He casually dropped into conversation that the pub was once a favourite haunt of Rob Roy himself. Which makes sense, because given the choice between a warm fire and ale or a damp cave full of spiders, I know where I'd be hiding too.

In fact, the pub's slogan—plastered proudly on a board outside—is: *"If it was good enough for Rob Roy, it's good enough for you."* Which, frankly, is a brilliant line and may be the first time I've agreed with marketing.

Apparently, the pub is also popular with big-name celebrities, and the barman whispered the names "Butler" and "Gerard" with the kind of reverence normally reserved for fine malts or footballers. I looked around the room for famous faces but was greeted only by other hikers who smelled faintly of damp and despair. So unless Gerard Butler had recently taken up stealth hiking and forgotten deodorant, I suspect we'd missed him.

Still, the barman was full of tales—and not just about whisky.

There have been countless reports of ghostly goings-on at the Drovers. Room six is famous for unexplained "orbs," which I think is ghost-hunter speak for "a dusty photo," and room two—yes, *that* room again—apparently plays host to the very same terrifying little girl, who has a charming habit of dripping icy water on guests while they sleep. Why? Well, legend has it she drowned in the nearby River Falloch while trying to retrieve her dropped doll. Frankly, I'd have let it go.

But none of that holds a candle to the pub's most legendary ghost: a young cattle drover named Angus.

Angus's tale is everything a proper ghost story should be—booze, betrayal, and violent revenge. Back in the 1700s, he was heading south with a herd of cattle, taking a break at the Drovers to enjoy a pint (or twelve) and maybe a bit of companionship. He drank the place dry, passed out, and woke up the next morning to find that rival clans had stolen *every single cow*.

This would have been bad enough had the

cattle been his. They were not. Angus was merely the courier. The bovine equivalent of Evri. Unfortunately, his Highland chieftain was not a man known for his understanding nature. In fact, he was more of a "kill everyone and marry your fiancée" kind of boss. Which is exactly what he did. Angus's entire family were slaughtered, and his bride-to-be was taken as a prize.

So Angus did what any vengeful Scot with a broken heart and no HR department would do: he returned to the Drovers with a plan. He would wait until the rival clan were well-oiled on whisky and then leap from hiding to stab the lot of them. Efficient. Dramatic. Blood-soaked.

Except someone rumbled him.

Instead of exacting his revenge, Angus was dragged outside to a tree behind the pub, strung up like a side of beef, and gutted alive. Slow, painful, and not the kind of TripAdvisor review the pub would want highlighted.

Ever since, people have claimed to see a lone figure wandering the nearby hills in all weathers —searching for his lost cattle, his honour, and possibly a pint to take the edge off.

By the time the barman finished his tale, I'd developed a healthy number of goosebumps and a very sudden need for the loo. I shuffled off toward the toilets, reassuring myself that ghosts aren't real and that even if they were, they definitely don't hang around urinals.

I still kept my eyes mostly closed, just in case.

If I *had* opened them, I might have noticed something familiar about the interior. The Drovers Inn featured in *Cloud Atlas*, a Tom Hanks film from a few years ago. Apparently, one of the fight scenes was shot right here, probably on the very floor we were currently dripping rainwater onto. I made a mental note to rewatch it later in the name of "research," though I suspect I'd still be none the wiser.

We stepped back outside into the warm afternoon sun and made our way over to the large marquee pitched beside the pub. It looked like it had been hastily assembled for outdoor drinking during the pandemic—or possibly as overflow for when the ghosts fancied a pint. Either way, we grabbed a table in the shade, and I wandered off to get a couple of drone shots of the pub, thinking I might as well immortalise the place from above before we moved on.

I didn't get very far.

Behind me, I heard a burst of snorting laughter —the unmistakable sound of two grown men reverting into 12-year-olds. Rob and Chris were calling me back, barely able to speak, and waving their phones around like they'd just discovered fire.

Naturally, I assumed they'd spotted something

interesting. A wild animal, maybe. A famous actor. A UFO, even.

Nope. It was my backside.

Or more accurately, what remained of my trousers. Rob was doubled over with laughter, his camera trained squarely on the gaping rip across the top of my right bum cheek. Apparently, I'd been strutting around like a budget Chippendale all day, blissfully unaware.

The tear stretched from waistband to almost mid-thigh—more of a trouser canyon than a split. Thankfully, my boxers were doing a sterling job of preserving my modesty, but only just. The only thing stopping this scene from becoming an actual crime was a thin strip of cotton and an overcast sky.

I was going to tell Rob to "go take a hike," but, well… that's literally what we were doing.

By now, he was hysterical. I mean full-on, tears-down-the-face, clutching-the-ribs, wheezing hysteria. Chris joined in too, because of course he did, and once I saw the photo, even I had to admit it was objectively funny.

Mystery solved: *that's* why everyone we passed had been smirking at me. And here I'd been thinking it was my rugged charm.

I tried to piece together when it had happened and remembered that ripping sound earlier in the day, when I'd shuffled down some rocks on my backside like a pensioner descending a water slide. That had been hours ago. Meaning I'd been airing my tartan cargo bay to every walker, goat, and ghost we'd passed.

I had no spare trousers. No needle, no thread, no dignity. Just a stiff breeze and a newfound appreciation for thick underwear. With no other option, I shrugged, accepted my fate, and prepared to moon my way to Crianlarich.

Besides, there were still miles to cover. The sun was arcing westward, and so—resisting the urge to fashion a curtain from the pub marquee—we bid farewell to our new best friend behind the bar, returned our glasses, and set off once again.

Naturally, we sang as we walked. *You take the high road and I'll take the low road...* We were almost in tune. Almost.

We retraced our steps past Beinglas Campsite, where we paused to top up our water bottles and —because we'd already earned it—grabbed an ice cream. By now, the sun was blazing down like it had just remembered it was summer. Which brought up the eternal walking dilemma: which is worse—being soaking wet, or slowly roasted in your own sweat like a walking haggis?

The trail doesn't officially go through the campsite, but the owners have cleverly built a little café right next to the path. Business was booming, and the smell of chips and bacon wafted over the picnic tables like a siren's song. Most people had dogs, which told me they were probably just out for a short jaunt, rather than three days of pants-related public embarrassment like yours truly.

Once hydrated, sugared up, and no longer entirely angry at the sun, we slung our packs on and continued our slow northern trudge. The path curled around the landscape like it had too much time on its hands, winding gently above the River Falloch, which sparkled below like it hadn't tried to drown a ghost girl earlier.

There were more walkers now—cheerful, smiling, all offering hearty greetings as if this sort of thing was actually enjoyable. And, in a way, it was.

There's something about being outside—properly outside—that straightens out the knots in your brain. Even when it's raining. Especially when it's raining, actually. The woods, the fresh air, the silence interrupted only by birds, wind, and the occasional scream of someone discovering a midge nest in their beard… it all works wonders.

It somehow reminded me of a winter trip to the coast with my son, when we built a snowman on the beach during a freak blizzard. Utterly surreal, completely freezing, but still one of the best memories I've got.

Multi-day walking trips like this, though—they

take it to another level. They unhook you from the real world. No emails. No pings. No social media algorithms trying to sell you trousers that *aren't* split open.

Out here, with no signal and no reason to check your phone except for taking blurry photos of trees, you remember how nice it is not to be reachable. The girls knew to meet us at Bridge of Orchy tomorrow evening, so there was nothing else we *needed* to do or *needed* to know.

For the first time in ages, we were truly off-grid. Free. And OK, yes—one of us had a torn backside flapping in the breeze—but what's a little accidental indecent exposure between friends?

The track leading away from the campsite was, quite frankly, a delight. After miles of foot-wrecking goat trails and root-infested lochside slogs, this was basically the West Highland Autobahn. It was wide enough for a car, flat enough for optimism, and mercifully free of anything trying to kill your ankles.

Even better, it meant we could finally walk three abreast like some sort of rugged Scottish boy band —if they'd swapped choreography for chafing. We could actually hold a conversation without shouting or turning our heads into the wind like confused spaniels.

Soon enough, the trees began to thin out and the landscape transformed into open moorland, the ground thick with ferns and tufts of heather —nature's version of shagpile carpet. The River Falloch gurgled somewhere below, and the noise of it began to grow louder with every step, which could only mean one thing: we were approaching the Falls of Falloch.

These falls are a bit of a hidden gem. By which I mean they're actually quite big, very noisy, and entirely unmissable... unless you're a West Highland Way walker, in which case you'll probably just barrel right past them because they're annoyingly out of sight behind some foliage. It's almost a rite of passage to miss them.

Luckily, we didn't. A natural viewpoint appeared, and we dropped our bags with a collective groan that said "blisters," and clambered down for a closer look. I kept well away from the water's edge because (a) I enjoy staying dry, and (b) I have the grace of a collapsing stepladder.

On the opposite bank was a car park and a gathering of people all jostling for selfies, most of them unaware that a moment of history was about to be made. That moment, of course, being Chris dropping his trousers.

Yes, we had arrived at our first *mooney* of the walk.

For those blessed enough to be unfamiliar with the term—and honestly, where have you been?— a *mooney* is the ancient and noble art of lowering one's trousers in public, purely for the sake of comedy. Not to be confused with streaking, which is athletic and alarming. A mooney is more... cheeky. Literally.

Chris didn't stop at the classic version either. No, he committed. Full exposure, both hands on hips, followed by a dramatic double slap to the buttocks and a bellowed "MOO-NEYYY!" across the river like a deranged foghorn.

People turned. Cameras clicked. Several children will now have questions for their parents.

One of the onlookers shouted, "How did you get over there?" and without missing a beat, Chris simply responded with another echoing, undeterred "MOO-NEYYY!"

Rob and I, being trapped on this side of the river with him, had little choice but to embrace the moment and enjoy the view. We just shrugged, nodded at the waterfall as if it were the most interesting thing in the world, and pretended we weren't part of whatever this was.

Important to clarify: when I say "we enjoyed the view," I mean *the actual waterfall*. Not the other one. Let's keep that crystal clear.

The pool beneath the falls is known—somewhat romantically—as Rob Roy's Bathtub, presumably where the legendary outlaw went for his weekly soak when he wasn't hiding in caves or sampling every whisky between here and Inverarnan. It's also where a man named William Murray almost drowned, and that would've been a bit awkward given everything he went on to achieve.

Good old Bill became one of Scotland's most revered mountaineers, nature writers and general all-round hardy type. He wrote extensively about the Highlands and mountaineering, and even did so twice. The first time was in a Nazi prison camp, on toilet paper, which the Gestapo then destroyed because apparently even fascists draw the line at unsolicited manuscripts.

Thankfully, he rewrote it after the war—presumably on actual paper this time—and also went on to pen a cracking biography of Rob Roy himself. So, all things considered, it's probably for the best that he didn't drown in that bathtub.

As we stood taking it all in, I couldn't help but think how spectacular the falls must be in spring, when the snowmelt turns them from "impressive" to "Niagara's angry cousin." Still, they weren't too shabby today either, even if the tourist-to-waterfall ratio was slightly off.

This stretch of the River Falloch is also popular with white-water rafters, many of whom apparently hurl themselves *over* the falls in what I can only assume is a very British attempt at natural selection. I watched the foaming cascade and mentally filed that under *Absolutely Not, Thank You Very Much*.

Instead, I stuck to what I'm good at: photographing nature and double-checking that Chris wasn't lurking in the background of any shots, preparing for *mooney number two*.

Eventually, the waterfalls behind us and the echoes of Chris's moon still lingering traumatically in the heads of several tourists, it was time to move on. The path welcomed us back with all the warmth of a grumpy sat-nav recalculating for the fifth time. It twisted and turned—up, down, left, right—like a particularly indecisive toddler, and we began to bake in the now merciless afternoon sun.

Ah yes, the great Scottish paradox. We'd spent days grumbling about rain, wet socks, and waterproofs that weren't, and now that we had actual sunshine, we were wilting like supermarket lettuce. As the sweat dribbled down my back, I caught myself fantasising about drizzle. Maybe even a light gale. Be careful what you wish for, they say—and for once, "they" were right.

We crossed a couple of wooden bridges, trudged along scenic slopes with glorious views stretching out in all directions, and were starting to think the worst of the day was behind us—until the trail did what all good trails do: it tried to kill us.

There, smack in the middle of our route, was a bridge—or more accurately, the ghost of one. It had clearly decided that life in the Highlands just wasn't worth it and had washed away in some dramatic weather-related tantrum. A helpful sign had been plonked beside the wreckage, suggesting a detour up the hill.

Because nothing says "easy, gentle walking route" like an emergency reroute that involves vertical climbing.

So up we went… for about three minutes.

That's when a group of walkers we'd seen earlier suddenly vanished off into the trees where the dead bridge lay. Moments later, like some sort of magical hiking portal, they re-emerged on the other side of the stream, dry and triumphant, as if to say, "Yes, you *can* ignore signs and live to tell the tale."

Naturally, we decided to follow their example.

What we found wasn't exactly a river. More of an enthusiastic stream, really—but one that still looked determined enough to carry off anyone not paying full attention. Perched beside it were a mature couple, mid-strip, removing socks and shoes with the seriousness of someone preparing for keyhole surgery.

We thought this was a touch dramatic, but who were we to judge? We'd seen Chris's bare backside in high definition not thirty minutes earlier.

Chris, being the wiry goat that he is, made the crossing look easy. He sprang from rock to rock like he'd been raised in a quarry, and made it to the other side without so much as a wobble. He was also, it must be said, beginning to develop a distinctive Highland musk. Somewhere between "outdoor adventurer" and "forgotten cheese."

I went next, adopting a more cautious, pilgrim-style approach, using my walking sticks like I was about to ski-jump into the afterlife. One of the rocks shifted beneath me, and for a brief, cinematic moment, I saw my life flash before my eyes—or at least the inevitable viral video footage that would follow.

With one final, glorious lunge, I leapt to safety. Slightly damp, slightly panicked, but upright. My shoes were wet but still keeping my socks dry, which felt like a minor miracle considering the growing ventilation hole in the right one.

Rob, meanwhile, was deep in conversation with the couple, who were now down to their ankles and contemplating whether to remove trousers entirely. I took out my phone—not out of concern, but because I was banking on a comedy pratfall that could earn me £250 and a clip on *You've Been Framed*. Tragically, Rob made it across in one piece, denying me both a payout and the sweet schadenfreude of watching him flounder like a soggy Labrador.

We waved the couple farewell—though they were still only half-dressed—and continued on.

Not long after, we paused for a quick look up toward the western slopes of Glen Falloch, where an ancient monolith stood out from the hills like a mislaid bit of Stonehenge. This was Clach nam Breatann—the Stone of the Britons. Allegedly, it once marked the boundary between the Britons and the Picts. Or possibly the Scots and the Britons. Or maybe the Picts and the marketing department of Historic Scotland.

There's also a theory it might be the Stone of Minuirc, marking the site of a battle so obscure that even the people who fought in it probably forgot what they were fighting about halfway through.

Still, it was old, it was mysterious, and it was far enough up the hill that none of us had any interest in climbing up to poke it. We admired it from a safe distance, nodded respectfully in its direction, and then got back to the more pressing business of not dying from sunstroke.

Soon enough we reached the hamlet—if you can call it that—of Derrydaroch. A single, lopsided cottage stood like it had just been asked to name all seven dwarves and given up halfway through. It looked like the sort of place that might once have housed a crofter, a goat, and possibly a ghost. Whether anyone actually lived there now was hard to tell. If they did, they were either asleep, invisible, or pretending not to be in.

This was also the spot where we finally crossed the River Falloch, courtesy of the Royal Engineers and their 1990s-era bridge. A lovely little metal plaque stood proudly bolted to the side, announcing that this fine bit of craftsmanship was brought to us by people who, unlike us, actually knew what they were doing. So it was slightly concerning, then, to be greeted immediately by a big yellow sign declaring the bridge to be dangerous. I mean, which was it? A proud feat of engineering or a death trap with delusions of grandeur?

We decided the sign was probably just there to keep the tourists on their toes and marched across anyway, testing every step like it might explode.

Now on the river's north bank, we carried on eastward, our merry little band of misfits sandwiched between the river on one side and the West Highland railway line on the other. Just beyond that lay the A82—the main road running up through this neck of the Highlands, which may as well have been a six-lane motorway given how often we'd been reduced to tiptoeing along goat paths.

Then came the moment we'd all been waiting for—well, *I* had, anyway. A sudden downhill jog in the trail brought us to a tunnel. Not a normal tunnel, mind you. This one was... petite. Let's say vertically challenged. It slithered beneath the railway in a way that made it very clear it had *not* been built with human passage in mind.

That's because it wasn't. This was a sheep creep.

Yes, a tunnel designed specifically for livestock. Sheep, in fact. Not big sheep either—your standard issue, knee-height, confused-looking, woolly fart machines. Certainly not a place for grown men with backpacks, bad knees, and dignity issues. Or, in Rob's case, grown men who were approximately the size of a double wardrobe.

Now, as has already been said, Rob, bless him, is a big unit. He towers well over six feet and comes with the sort of broad-shouldered frame that makes shop mannequins weep with inadequacy. And here he was, faced with a tunnel that could barely accommodate the average hobbit.

Never ones to miss a comedy opportunity, Chris and I whipped out our phones and started filming immediately. Not to help, obviously. Just to immortalise the moment for posterity—or YouTube, whichever came first. Rob, bent double like a man searching for his keys in a crawl space, edged into the tunnel. It wasn't graceful. It wasn't elegant. It was like trying to post a fridge through a letterbox.

He grunted. He groaned. His rucksack scraped every inch of the ceiling, and we could hear him muttering something about being wedged. I half expected to hear the words "send help" echoing back down the tunnel. To his credit, he made it through—eventually—though I'm fairly sure there's still DNA of his left shoulder embedded in the roof somewhere.

On the other side, Rob was greeted by yet *another* tunnel—this one under the main road—but thankfully this one was built for cars and humans, so he could walk through it upright like a normal person. Which was disappointing. We'd really hoped for a sequel.

Between the tunnels, the path briefly joined a hilariously narrow strip of tarmac that had once been the main road around here. Honestly, I've seen wider bike lanes. The thought that people used to drive caravans along this road made me instantly want to locate the nearest pub and toast their bravery.

Popping out into the daylight again like three very sweaty moles, we found ourselves at the base of Glen Falloch's flanks, where the trail decided we hadn't had enough vertical punishment for one day and began dragging us uphill once more.

This section followed an old military road, part of a vast network built across the Highlands by the ever-diligent General George Wade—known to his mates, presumably, as "Wade the Paver." After the first Jacobite Rebellion in 1715, the English looked north and thought, "You know what we need? Roads. Lots of roads. And bridges. And maybe a few forts while we're at it."

So they dispatched General Wade to knock Scotland into something resembling submission—or at the very least, accessibility. He got to work building a spider's web of infrastructure so troops could march quickly from one dramatic mutiny to the next.

Now, while Wade gets all the headlines, the real graft was done by Major William Caulfeild (yes, with a weird spelling—probably to make him harder to Google). Caulfeild knocked up over 700 miles of road and more than 600 bridges. Which, frankly, makes me tired just typing it.

And here we were, 300 years later, sweating and swearing our way up one of his more scenic contributions to the cause. I'm sure he'd be thrilled to know it was now being used by three middle-aged idiots, one of whom had recently torn the backside out of his trousers and another who'd just survived a sheep tunnel by the skin of his rucksack.

Thanks, George. Or William. Or both. Much appreciated.

The path mellowed as we approached Crianlarich, following a gentler sweep through the valley—clearly designed by someone who believed that not every stretch of the Highlands needed to punish you. We began our slow descent towards the village, hopeful that a decent night's sleep awaited, ideally somewhere that didn't involve midges, collapsing tents, or Rob snoring like a chainsaw trapped in a wardrobe.

We weren't alone on this final stretch—other walkers had emerged, blinking into the sunlight like confused wildlife. One couple we passed were clearly having a *blister situation*—the kind where toes look like overinflated cocktail sausages. Rob, ever the humanitarian (at least when it comes to other people's feet), offered up a few Compeeds, which they gratefully accepted. He probably only did it so he could dramatically say "Keep the change" and pretend he was in a Western.

Shortly afterwards, we stumbled across the infamous camping chair. Yes, *that* chair—an unexpected roadside attraction that's somehow become a bit of a cult icon on the Way. Apparently, there's usually an honesty box there too, which adds a sort of mystical, Highland vending-machine charm to the scene. But today? No box. Just a lonely, slightly weathered seat and a sense of unmet potential. We carried on, feeling mildly cheated but not quite sure why.

Leaving the open valley behind, we passed through Bogle Glen and reached Crianlarich Crossroads. We ducked through a sizeable kissing gate and an even larger deer fence—because clearly the local deer are on steroids—and spotted what can only be described as *The Promised Land*.

A perfect little wild campsite awaited us: flat

ground, a campfire pit, an actual wooden bench —luxury by Highland standards. All thoughts of trudging into the village and pretending to enjoy civilisation vanished immediately. Packs off. Boots off. Spirits up.

We congratulated each other on surviving another day in the wilds without any limbs detaching or anyone being eaten by goats. For a blissful moment, we just sat, basking in the golden glow of a Highlands sunset and pretending we were rugged adventurers rather than middle-aged blokes with questionable knees.

Then Rob sprang into action.

Now, he might not be a Nobel laureate or a rocket scientist, but give the man a camp stove and a packet of mince, and he turns into Gordon Ramsay's gruff, slightly beardier cousin. He fired up his trusty liquid-fuel stove—which we'd learned long ago was far more reliable than the butane cans that like to evaporate in your rucksack for no reason whatsoever—and soon had chilli con carne and rice bubbling away like a culinary cauldron.

While Rob performed his nightly miracle, Chris and I wrestled with the tent. Somehow, we got it up without needing first aid or counselling, sorted the sleeping gear, and plonked ourselves on the bench, faces full of admiration and mouths full of chilli. The sunset behind us turned a fiery shade of apocalypse as we ate, the kind of sky that makes you feel tiny and alive and also slightly worried about spontaneous combustion.

We were careful not to trail too much dirt into the tent because, as every experienced camper knows, one careless bootprint on the first night is all it takes to grow an entire allotment by the third. A clean tent may not be as comfy as a hotel room with a pool, but it's infinitely better than accidentally sprouting courgettes between your sleeping bags.

A pair of joggers passed by without so much as a grunt of acknowledgement—possibly because they'd spotted my ripped trousers and feared we were some kind of feral gang. Then came three cyclists, who at least had the decency to say hello, though I suspect this was only because we were watching them wrestle their bikes through the kissing gate like it was a circus act involving unwilling giraffes.

Next, an elderly gent approached at that weird pace that's half-walk, half-sprint and full midlife crisis. He stopped for a chat and asked if we'd seen a water source. We hadn't, so he said he'd continue on to Herive Burn, a couple of miles up the trail. We offered him water, which he politely declined —probably because he didn't fancy our sweaty rucksack-flavoured tap water.

With him gone, the woods fell silent. We sat

back down, legs throbbing, faces smudged with soot and smugness. Rob polished off the last of the coffee, and I launched the drone for a final, swooping panorama of our perfect little camp. I got some lovely footage—mountains glowing in the dying light, smoke curling up from the fire, Chris scratching his arse like a confused bear.

Then we waited.

We knew what was coming.

The sun dipped below the treeline, and the air cooled.

The great midge countdown had begun...

We didn't have to wait long. By 8pm, the midges were out in force, forming tiny, angry clouds that immediately set about making our lives miserable. Our solution? Fire. Glorious, smoky, eye-watering fire.

We vanished into the woods like foraging cavemen, on the hunt for anything flammable. Rob, true to form, took the opportunity to nearly torch his own face by lighting the fire with a dash of stove fuel. A small price to pay for an inferno that would hopefully keep the bloodthirsty horde at bay. Once lit, the fire crackled away nicely, belching out enough smoke to deter midges, mosquitoes, and possibly even passing aircraft.

Unfortunately, further wood-gathering missions revealed slim pickings. Clearly this campsite had seen plenty of action before. What it *did* have, however, was pine cones—an absolute carpet of them. So we ditched firewood and pivoted to pine cone pyromania, collecting bucketloads of the stuff.

Of course, while sniffing out cones, we also found a few unsavoury spots where previous campers had clearly taken care of... other business. I shall spare you the details, but let's just say some areas of the forest were henceforth designated no-go zones.

Still, the cones did the job, and the fire stayed lit. As the light began to fade, Rob pulled out his hip flask like a cowboy at a campfire and offered up a celebratory nip of something strong enough to dissolve tooth enamel. I accepted, obviously.

Emboldened (and mildly pickled), I wandered back into the woods solo to grab more cones. It was technically still daylight, but under the thick canopy it felt like midnight. I kept telling myself it was probably just a squirrel... but when a twig snapped behind me, I set a new land speed record getting back to camp. I didn't stop until I'd had another nip—strictly medicinal.

As is tradition, a tiny splash of whisky combined with a whole day of hiking meant we were soon tipsy enough to declare the fire a makeshift nightclub. There we were: three middle-aged men dancing around the flames like druids who'd lost the plot. When a couple of late-arriving hikers stumbled into our little bacchanalia, they took one look at us, declined our invitation to join the rave, and wisely continued on to Crianlarich. Can't imagine why.

They did mention having two more friends behind them, so we promised to point the stragglers in the right direction. One arrived not long after, looking like he'd just crawled out of a hedge backwards, muttered a few exhausted words, and shuffled down the path. The final member was still missing as darkness really took hold and the stars began to appear—sparkling companions who, unlike my tent-mates, didn't fart in their sleep.

Just as we were about to turn in, we heard voices again. The original duo, plus straggler, had clearly decided that walking into the pitch-black woods was a terrible idea and came back to set up camp near us. They didn't seem up for chatting —possibly because they'd just spent an hour watching three idiots dance around a pine cone inferno—but we gave them a polite wave, collected more fuel for the fire, and headed to bed.

Now, let me explain something very important: my sleeping bag is a *mummy bag*. For the uninitiated, this means you enter it like a caterpillar and zip yourself into a synthetic tomb. It's wonderfully warm, but it comes with one small design flaw. The urgency of your need to pee is directly linked to how thoroughly zipped in you are, how cold the outside world is, and how many layers of clothing you're wearing. Luckily for me, it was unseasonably warm and I wasn't dressed like an Arctic explorer, so I had a decent shot at surviving the night without a 3am escape mission.

I lay back, listening to the unfamiliar sounds of the forest—rustling trees, distant murmurs, the occasional snore—and gave thanks that it wasn't raining. I always end up on the side of the tent that leaks, no matter which side that is.

Finally, just as sleep began to win, the last member of the wandering quartet rolled in. We could hear them regrouping outside, muttering about how hard the day had been, how wrecked they all were, and how they definitely needed a day off.

I couldn't agree more.

And then I was gone.

Crianlarich To Bridge Of Orchy

What happens in the tent stays in the tent.

Unknown

We woke around six to a beautiful, peaceful silence—ruined only by the rhythmic chainsaw hum of four comatose lads snoring in stereo from tents all around us. Somehow, they'd managed to strategically position themselves for maximum acoustical reach. Impressive, really.

Peeking out of the tent flap, I saw what promised to be another glorious weather day. Blue skies. Not a single cloud in sight. Which is all lovely, of course, until you remember that walking in direct sun is basically like roasting yourself alive in a waterproof jacket. Still, it was chilly for now, so we pretended to be optimistic.

Morning routines kicked in like clockwork. Rob, camp chef and fire hazard extraordinaire, brewed up some breakfast and coffee, while Chris and I packed away the tent and sleeping gear. All this noise—zips zipping, pans clanging, us muttering about socks—was apparently not enough to disturb the human walruses around us. The lads snored on, completely undisturbed, which was oddly impressive. They must've been absolutely shattered. Or dead. We didn't check.

By 8am, we were good to go. After one final sweep to make sure we hadn't left any souvenirs or half-buried socks behind, we were back on the trail.

Naturally, this meant one thing: a massive hill. Because why ease into the day with a nice gentle stroll when you can instead begin by crawling up the other side of Bogle Glen, lungs on fire, legs screaming, and morale somewhere near your ankles? I'm beginning to think Scotland designed this trail like an army boot camp.

There's an argument to be made that starting with a steep climb is a good way to "warm up." There's also an argument that it's a horrendous way to begin a day. I remain undecided, mostly because I was too busy gasping for air to form a coherent opinion.

This time, though, it wasn't me lagging behind —it was Rob. Possibly still digesting breakfast. Possibly reconsidering his life choices. Either way, I enjoyed my brief moment of not-being-last while it lasted.

We regrouped at the top of the first hill section and stumbled upon what would've made an absolutely perfect campsite. Tucked in neatly between trees was just enough flat space for a single tent and, remarkably, a picnic bench. Yes, a full-size wooden picnic bench. How it got there is one of life's great unsolved mysteries, because I certainly wouldn't fancy carrying one up that slope. Whoever did it deserves a medal. Or a therapist.

As we stood catching our breath, the view below us opened up into something properly breathtaking. Low clouds hovered still and silent in the glens beneath, while the morning sun, hanging low over the eastern peaks, blazed directly into our eyes like some celestial interrogation lamp.

It was shaping up to be another beautiful, ridiculous, soul-challenging sort of day.

From the lookout with the picnic bench to the land of Tolkien-esque forestry gloom, the path promptly vanished into the woods and became an endless game of "guess which way is up." Twisting and turning like a drunken snake, it threw us into a series of ups, downs, and just-for-fun side angles. I couldn't help but wonder how easy it would be to get hopelessly lost in here. If you wandered off the trail for even a minute, you'd probably end up starring in your own Blair Witch reboot. The conifers—planted in rows like a green army—were almost hypnotic, and the floor was as lumpy and welcoming as a bed of bricks. I began to suspect these trees were less "forest" and more "maze for the easily disoriented."

Deciding to avoid becoming a cautionary tale on a laminated warning poster, we stuck to the path and were rewarded with a peaceful little footbridge over Herive Burn. It looked like the kind of place that's perfect for refilling your water if you're the sort of person who forgets to hydrate, or just likes to play with filters and pretend to be Bear Grylls. I wasn't short on water, so the stream and its suspicious-looking rocks remained unbothered by me. Tyndrum, after all, wasn't that far off, and they probably had actual taps. Possibly even vending machines.

Post-burn, the trail kept on doing its slithering impression, until at last we joined a wider track that showed signs of human reason—mostly because it went downhill. To our right, faint sounds of traffic began to filter through the trees, which meant we were nearing the main road and civilisation, or at least what passed for it in this part of the Highlands.

We didn't burst out onto tarmac just yet, though. First, we emerged from the trees at a railway line, slipping beneath it via a perfectly functional but comically small viaduct. I say "viaduct" because it sounds grand, but really it was just a small underpass that didn't require us to crawl, which felt like a treat after Rob's Tunnel of Doom yesterday.

Then the forest began to loosen its grip, and we stumbled into a meadow. A lovely, innocent-looking field that would've been forgettable… if it weren't for what I saw glistening in the grass.

Spiderwebs. Everywhere.

Dozens of them at first, then as my eyes adjusted, hundreds. Maybe thousands. The morning dew had collected perfectly on each silken strand, making them stand out like a Halloween decoration budget gone rogue. It was breathtaking. Also slightly terrifying.

Now, I don't mind spiders—at least not until they're moving faster than me—but even I had to pause. My wife, however, would have burst into flames and run screaming into the trees. She's utterly petrified of spiders, even though in the UK, the worst most of them can do is give you a mildly annoying itch and maybe make you squeal in the shower.

People like to panic about the noble false widow spider, but even that requires some serious provoking before it'll even think about nibbling you. And let's be honest, any animal that comes from the Canary Islands is probably more interested in sunbathing than fighting. They've slowly been making their way north, apparently, thanks to climate change. Which means that in a few years, Yorkshire might be their Ibiza, so it'll be safe up here for a while yet.

But back to our field of dreams and nightmares. The truth is, most of the UK's spiders—even the venomous ones—aren't out to get you. Unless, of course, you're crawling into your tent after dark and accidentally sandwich one against your face. But that's a risk we all take in the great outdoors, and if you're reading this, you've either accepted that... or you've already screamed and thrown the book out the window.

Shortly after playing "Spot the Spider" in the meadow of nightmares, we made our way under the railway and popped out near the road—by which I mean *on* the road. And when I say road, I mean a narrow strip of tarmac masquerading as a Formula One test track, complete with blind bends in both directions.

There was no bridge, of course. That would've been too easy. So we stood there like startled ducks at the edge of a motorway, trying to gauge whether each fleeting gap in the traffic was a good time to cross or just an excellent opportunity to be flattened by an Audi. Naturally, as soon as one direction cleared, the other one roared into action, like they were working in shifts to make sure we stayed on the verge forever.

Eventually, and possibly with the blessing of some pagan hiking god, we darted across without anyone doing an impromptu hedgehog impression and slipped back into the relative safety of the trees on the other side. A newly laid path awaited us, skirting along the road and overlooking a wonderfully swampy forest—beautiful in a sort of "dinosaurs might reappear any second" way. It was all very peaceful, if you ignored the death-rattle of juggernauts behind the treeline.

Chris, naturally, was miles ahead by now, probably trying to find someone new to talk to about camping stoves. We followed in single file, weaving through the corridor of foliage until a small sign politely suggested we turn right and cross a bridge over the River Fillan.

Now, the River Fillan is one of those watercourses with a personality disorder. In this particular valley, it's called the Fillan. Further upstream it's the River Cononish, and downstream it transforms into the River Dochart. It's basically the Beyoncé of rivers—reinventing itself every few miles. This whole stretch, by the way, runs through Strath Fillan, with "strath" being the posh way of saying "wide and shallow valley." It's like a glen but without the drama. Unless you're the river, obviously.

We crossed the bridge and ambled toward Kirkton Farm, hoping to spot the ruins of St Fillan's Priory. But halfway through the meadow, an information board distracted us. It offered up mountain names and facts like some sort of scenic Wikipedia page nailed to a stick.

Most impressive on the list was Ben More, towering at 1,174 metres, or about 3,850 feet in English. It's significantly higher than Ben Lomond, and in fact, there's no higher land south of it in the whole of the UK. This makes it not only big, but smug about it too.

Naturally, this kind of altitude invited trouble. And sure enough, the board informed us that a Vickers Viscount airliner had crashed into Ben More back in 1973. It had taken off from Glasgow at 2:22pm, presumably hoping for a relaxing fifteen-minute test flight to make sure an earlier fault had been fixed. Ten minutes later, it had smashed into the side of the mountain, killing everyone on board.

The crash was blamed on pilot error—because of course it was—but the accident report hinted at something less convenient. Apparently, Glasgow airport staff had cleared the aircraft to fly at an altitude that was *obviously* far too low in this area. But hey, why let a bit of common sense get in the way of some finger-pointing?

The wreckage is still up there, too—just a hundred feet below the summit. If you're the kind of person who enjoys hiking up mountains to see twisted bits of 1970s fuselage, you'll find plenty of photos online to fuel your obsession.

We stood there for a moment in silence, gazing up at the hulking presence of Ben More in the distance, trying not to think too hard about tragic air disasters while wearing slightly sweaty hiking socks. Then we did what British people do best— we moved on and didn't talk about it.

We trudged on past Kirkton Farm, and almost immediately came across what was left of St Fillan's Priory—though "left" might be a bit generous. A couple of stones and a well-meaning information board was about all that remained, making it less of a priory and more of a vague suggestion.

St Fillan himself had apparently been a big deal once upon a time. An abbot from Fife, he eventually retired to this peaceful little valley where he made quite the name for himself as a miracle-working missionary and general fixer-of-broken-people. His party trick? Making his left arm glow. Yes, really. Not for signalling taxis or terrifying children at Halloween, but to help him write scripture in the middle of the night.

Now, why he didn't just wait until morning like a normal person or, I don't know, *light a candle*, remains one of history's great unsolved mysteries. Perhaps he just liked to show off. Either way, the image of him on the info board looked alarmingly like Chris, especially with the matching walking sticks. It was unsettling. If Chris starts glowing at any point, I'm out.

The priory itself had been established in 1318

by none other than Robert the Bruce, King of the Scots and all-round English-thrashing enthusiast. He built it as a big thank you to St Fillan, who he believed had helped him batter Edward II's army into submission at Bannockburn.

You see, Robert the Bruce brought a holy relic with him into battle: the *Mayne*—which, as it turns out, was actually St Fillan's arm bone. Presumably the magic, glow-in-the-dark one. I like to think he used it like a medieval lightsaber, swinging it around on horseback like a divine flail. Whether or not he actually clubbed any English soldiers with it remains unconfirmed, but the victory was so decisive that Bruce gave full credit to Fillan's detached limb. Take that, military strategy.

Before we moved on, I suggested a quick prayer to St Fillan—what with him also being the patron saint of the mentally ill and all. I felt that really captured the essence of our group. Chris laughed, but Rob looked oddly serious. Maybe he was just thinking about his home life.

Still, it got me wondering. Turns out there's a saint for just about everything nowadays. St Gummarus (a name that sounds like a sexually transmitted disease) is the patron saint of difficult marriages—one I'll be sure to mention to my wife at an appropriate and tactful time, like never. St Rita handles the impossible, so she's clearly got Rob's life on her rota. St Julian, for reasons no one can quite explain, is the patron saint of murderers.

Cheery.

But my absolute favourite? St Drogo—yes, really —is the patron saint of ugly people. You can't make this stuff up. Well, you *can*, but apparently the Vatican beat us to it.

There's more. St Barbara covers anything that explodes (ideal if your hobby is fireworks or landmines), while St Catherine is basically the miscellaneous drawer of the saint world. She covers single women, dying people, knife sharpeners, mechanics, philosophers, schoolchildren, and entire countries—including Greece and the Philippines. She's clearly on a zero-hours contract.

Eventually, it was time to stop loitering like a gang of suspicious historians and move on. We'd spent far too long discussing saints, bones, and dubious glowing appendages beside what was, if we're being honest, a priory in the same way a brick is a bungalow. Still, before we left, we nipped around the back to check out the small burial ground tucked just behind the ruins.

Another handy information board (someone, somewhere, is making a killing on those things) told us about a series of ancient stone slabs dating back to medieval times, adorned with engraved crosses. We found them easily enough and stood there admiring their quiet dignity—though I must admit, once you've seen one mossy cross slab, you've seen them all. The board also mentioned that similar slabs could be found in places like Fortingall, which rang a faint bell.

I'd actually been to Fortingall once, many moons ago, lured in by the promise of the famous tree said to be 3,000 years old. That's *almost* as old as Rob, though slightly more sprightly. Somehow, I'd missed the slabs entirely, which is the sort of thing that makes you question your attention span, or at least your ability to read signs.

We pushed on, the path winding gently through pleasant meadows that were bursting with hoofed locusts (sheep, remember?) bleating at us like some sort of woolly protest rally. The scenery was stunning: soft green fields framed by stern, handsome mountains that looked like they'd been placed there by someone with a decent sense of drama.

The temperature had crept up, and though it was still fairly pleasant, we paused to slap on some sun cream. I gave myself a mental high-five for bringing a hat—yet again proving that fashion and function are not always mutually exclusive, no matter what Chris says.

Soon we arrived at a farm-turned-campsite, where a woman of mature years was stood awkwardly in the middle of a field, phone pressed to her ear like a lighthouse searching for signal. Rob remarked that this was probably the only place she could get reception—and sure enough, she confirmed it with a laugh as we walked past.

It was then, of course, that I remembered the rather gaping hole in the back of my trousers. Until that point, I'd completely forgotten that I'd spent the last two days giving everyone behind me an unsolicited glimpse of my boxers. She laughed again, and I couldn't decide whether it was the phone call or my accidental exhibitionism.

The campsite was a tidy little place with triangular "camping pods"—which, let's be honest, are just wooden sheds that people pretend are luxurious. I wandered over to peer inside one out of sheer nosiness, only to find that it was, in fact, occupied. The person within didn't seem remotely bothered, but I mumbled a flustered apology and made a swift retreat, trying to look like someone who definitely wasn't creeping around people's holiday homes uninvited.

The path led us next to the Holy Pool, also known as St Fillan's Pool, which sounds serene and spiritual until you find out what actually went on there. What looks like just a pleasant bend in the river was once the setting for a sort of medieval obstacle course for the mentally ill.

You see, St Fillan—our favourite glow-armed saint—was not just the patron saint of the mentally unstable but also the apparent inventor of traumatic therapy. In the olden days, sufferers were dragged here for treatment, which involved diving to the bottom of the pool to retrieve stones as proof they'd done so. These stones were then lovingly plopped onto nearby cairns. Sounds reasonable so far, right? Well, hold onto your loincloth.

Next, they were stripped naked (obviously), tied up in the local church or priory, and made to spend the night beneath a suspended bell. If by morning they'd managed to escape, congratulations! You were cured. If not—well, better luck next time. Repeat until sane or broken beyond repair. As I stood there swatting midges and staring at the pool, I figured the insects alone were enough to induce a breakdown. We moved on before my own mental state took a dive.

Passing under the main road, we followed the River Fillan for a while, enjoying a bit of shade from the trees, the water babbling nearby in that calming way rivers do before something ridiculous inevitably happens. Sure enough, after an arched stone bridge and a bit more pleasant meandering, we stumbled upon yet another information board —because what's a walk in Scotland without being educated against your will?

This one declared the site of the Battle of Dalrigh, which I'll admit I'd never heard of. But don't worry—I'm now an expert.

It all kicked off in 1306, which was a chaotic

year for Robert the Bruce, the Macdougalls, and anyone else with a sword and a bad attitude. At the centre of it all were Robert the Bruce, a rival named John Comyn, a fella called John Balliol, and a truly epic amount of grudges.

Comyn, who was in the Balliol camp (literally and politically), wasn't exactly Bruce's biggest fan. Bruce, not known for being chill about these things, invited Comyn for a cosy little meeting at Greyfriars Church in Dumfries. What happened inside is unclear, but one thing is for certain— Comyn left in a box. Or at least he would've, if boxes were a thing in 1306.

Shortly after this ecclesiastical stabbing, Bruce crowned himself King of the Scots. Unfortunately, assassinating one of the most powerful men in Scotland tends to make enemies, and the Macdougalls, who were basically Team Comyn, decided Bruce had to go. Enter John of Argyll, Macdougall clan chief and general bringer of beef, who ambushed Bruce here at Dalrigh, hoping to finish the job the English had started.

They almost managed it too, but Bruce narrowly escaped, helped along by the Macdonalds—sworn enemies of the Macdougalls and presumably always up for a bit of anti-Macdougall mischief. Bruce regrouped at record speed, then crushed the Macdougalls at the Pass of Brander two years later, dishing out revenge like a Game of Thrones character with a grudge and a broadsword.

When Bruce won big at Bannockburn in 1314, he carved up the Macdougall lands and handed big chunks over to his supporters, especially the Macdonalds. Which must have felt very satisfying indeed—like changing your will just to cut out your least favourite cousin.

Now, while Robert the Bruce is rightly celebrated as a Scottish hero, things get confusing when Hollywood sticks its nose in. Most people think of *Braveheart* when they hear his name, which is hilarious because *Braveheart* is actually about William Wallace. The filmmakers just nicked the title because it sounded cool—and historically accurate titles like *Tall Hairy Bloke With a Sword* don't sell tickets.

The film plays fast and loose with the facts: that whole "right of first night" nonsense, where mediaeval nobles can have sex with any new bride, has no real evidence, Wallace's dad was probably alive during the rebellion, and the face paint and kilts? He was 1,000 years too late for blue warpaint and 500 years too early for tartan. But still, it looks amazing and Mel Gibson gives it his all—even if his Scottish accent should be reported to UNESCO as a war crime.

Perhaps the most offensive bit of creative licence, though, was portraying Robert the Bruce as a traitor. He absolutely wasn't, and if you're ever in a Scottish pub, I suggest you don't bring it up unless you're fond of dental work.

Anyway, there's not much left to see here today. The site is now part of a nature reserve, and you'd never know it was once the scene of such drama, bloodshed, and strategic double-crossing. The only real clue is in the name—Dalrigh, which translates as "the king's field." Presumably not a reference to Robert's gardening habits.

We wandered on through meadows and woodland, all feeling quite smug about the fact that we were finally closing in on Tyndrum— land of promised food, beverages, and possibly a toilet that didn't involve crouching near a pine cone. We could just about hear traffic humming away beyond the trees, but the road itself remained hidden. That was, of course, until we rounded a bend and—ta-da!—were rewarded not with a scenic viewpoint or a pub, but another information board. Because nothing says "wilderness escape" like surprise educational signage.

This one treated us to the legend of the *Lochan of the Lost Sword*, which sounds like a straight-to-DVD fantasy film starring Sean Bean and some really questionable CGI. According to the tale, after getting his backside handed to him at Dalrigh, Robert the Bruce legged it past this small lochan and chucked his sword—and presumably anything else remotely heavy—into the water to make a speedier getaway.

Apparently, one particularly determined

Macdougall soldier had a pop at Bruce, grabbing his cloak in an attempt to yank him from his horse, but Bruce responded by stabbing him. Fair. Unfortunately, in the process, Bruce lost his cloak and a shiny brooch, which later became known as *The Brooch of Lorn*. The Macdougalls kept it as a sort of murder souvenir until 1647, when Clan Campbell—never ones to miss a bit of looting—burned down Gylen Castle and nicked it.

The brooch then reappeared in the 1800s, found by Major Campbell of Bragleen (a less dastardly Campbell, apparently), who had the decency to give it back to the Macdougalls in 1824. Probably in his will. Possibly after being haunted. Understandably paranoid that someone would nick it again, the Macdougalls kept it hidden until 1956, when they showed it off to the Queen, who presumably dropped in to Oban for a bit of tea and historical bling.

Now, this is where the experts get involved and ruin the fun. Those pesky historians claim the brooch is actually from the 15th century—well over a hundred years *after* Bruce died in 1329—which means he couldn't possibly have dropped it, lost it, or impaled anyone while wearing it. But don't worry, another group of experts say the *stone* in the brooch might actually be older, and it's just the mount that's from the wrong time. So the brooch might be kind of real. Sort of. In a vibe-based, emotionally resonant way. Like a historical cover version.

Putting the romanticised relic behind us, we carried on into increasingly sparse woods, with the roar of traffic now getting louder and less charming by the minute. This had to mean Tyndrum was close—possibly close enough for a hot meal and a smug sit-down at the famous *Green Welly Stop*, which is either a legendary hiker's haven or a motorway services with a wardrobe theme. I'll let you decide.

We entered a heather-clad moor that turned out to be a "community woodland"—which is basically a fancy way of saying "lovely patch of trees that belongs to everyone but gets looked after by the same three people". The paths were smooth, the heather was blooming in pink and purple, and the whole place had a bit of a fairyland vibe. Signs promised us pine martens, red squirrels, and majestic red deer. Naturally, we saw absolutely none of these things.

We *did* see a black grouse, though. It burst out of the heather with all the subtlety of a chainsaw and nearly gave Rob a coronary on the spot. He leapt three feet in the air, which nearly finished me and Chris off from laughter. The grouse, satisfied with its emotional destruction, flapped off into the distance.

The trees began to fade entirely now, and soon we found ourselves at the derelict remains of what used to be a lead smelter. Not much was left except a crumbling stone column that looked more like a ruined pizza oven than a major part of industrial history, but it was marked on the map, so we nodded respectfully.

From here, the path followed a cheerful little stream into the outskirts of Tyndrum proper. We passed a campsite with a very unwelcoming sign declaring that no campers were being accepted this year—something we assumed was COVID-related, though for all we knew it might just be a "no scruffy walkers" policy.

Still, the village was now in sight. We'd made it. Robert the Bruce had his brooch stolen, Rob had been assaulted by a grouse, and I was still strutting around with a bum-flap in my trousers—but somehow, we were all still alive and ready for a sit down and something edible.

We emerged onto a road in the village itself, not far from the western train station—yes, *western*, because in a move of logistical overkill, Tyndrum has not one, but *two* railway lines slicing through it, and therefore two separate stations. This one trundles through scenic Glen Lochy, flirts with the River Orchy, then makes a dramatic run through the Pass of Brander—where, you may recall, the Macdougalls had their historically inconvenient demise—before curling round the coast to Oban, aka the Gateway to the Isles, aka "the place you go when you fancy a ferry and a fight with a seagull."

At the other end of the village lies the rather more glamorous West Highland Line, which bolts north toward Bridge of Orchy, Rannoch Moor and Corrour Station before swinging west through Spean Bridge and ending up at Fort William. Corrour, incidentally, is the highest train station in the UK and, unless you've got a particular fondness for 20-mile slogs through mountainous nothingness, it can *only* be reached by train. Trainspotting fans might recall this is where Renton and the boys jumped off to prove how rugged and outdoorsy they were, before promptly realising that the wilderness is, in fact, mostly bog.

Anyway, we were soon marching along the main road into the bustling heart of Tyndrum—a word I'm using loosely here, as 'bustling' meant we passed more than three people in a row. Our eyes were immediately drawn to The Tyndrum Inn and the tantalising promise of a cold pint glistening in the sun. Without hesitation, we dumped our packs beside the beer garden benches and strode into the lobby like conquering heroes... only to find every door beyond that was firmly locked. A pub with commitment issues, it seemed.

Undeterred and mildly confused, we sauntered up the road to the *Green Welly Stop*, which mercifully *was* open. It turns out that while pubs may be mysterious and aloof, the Welly is always ready for action. Judging by the constant crunch of gravel under tyres, the car park out back was doing a roaring trade. Families sprawled across picnic tables, ice creams in hand, kids running amok, dogs trying to steal chips—Tyndrum was positively alive. We nabbed the last free bench, beating a pair of pensioners by sheer luck and questionable morals. Had it come down to it, I probably *would* have rugby-tackled them. Bench survival is a serious business.

Chris, always the self-elected Quartermaster General, wandered into the shop and returned with sandwiches, cakes, and drinks for us to squabble over. After days of peaceful woodland and quiet trails, Tyndrum was practically a sensory overload—a hyperactive metropolis where the currency was cola and the soundtrack was screaming children.

Speaking of which, the kid at the next table gave us a solid moment of joy when he opened his bottle of Coke and triggered what can only be described as a cola-based explosion. It drenched him, his family, and even their poor dog, who looked as if this was not the life he had signed up for. I did what any good-hearted person would do: laughed, *then* handed them some wet wipes. Public service with a side of Schadenfreude.

The Green Welly is a bit of a cult icon on the West Highland Way, and after our failed pub escapade, I was starting to feel glad the inn had been closed. Everyone talks about the Welly— some moan about the prices, but let's be honest, this place is basically a motorway service station with better scenery and fewer toilet queues. It's remote, it's well-stocked, and the price of a sausage roll includes a side of logistical nightmare, so you can't grumble too much.

The whole operation began back in 1965 when Betty and Les Gosden thought, "Let's sell up everything, move to the middle of nowhere, and open a shop." You know, as you do. Apparently, Les had clocked that Tyndrum was impossible to bypass without falling off a cliff or fighting a highland cow, so he reckoned the location was perfect. He wasn't wrong. What started as a humble shop and post office has since exploded into a Highland mega-stop, still recognisably the same old building if you squint, but now expanded to the point where it could probably host the Olympics.

I had a nosey around the gift shop but quickly realised that I didn't want to carry tartan-themed fridge magnets or humorous tea towels for the next umpteen miles. So instead, we tucked into our food, used the toilets like the civilised animals we pretend to be, and then reluctantly got ready to hit the trail once more.

One final wistful glance at the benches (and a quick check that the pensioners weren't plotting revenge), and off we went—re-caffeinated, slightly sugared-up, and at least one of us still wearing trousers with a hole in the arse.

A fingerpost pointed us out of Tyndrum at the other end of the village, though unfortunately it was also pointing uphill, which felt rather rude. Still, we had no choice, so off we trudged, dragging ourselves away from the civilised comforts of sandwiches, flushing toilets and benches not made of moss.

Just as we were passing the village boundary, we stopped to admire some impressively carved wooden animals that someone with far too much time and a dangerous level of chainsaw skill had sculpted out of tree stumps. These made for a convenient excuse to stop and catch our breath without admitting we were knackered.

Once our heart rates had returned to something vaguely human, we continued uphill, following a path that loosely traced the route of a nearby river. As we ascended, we spotted several people actually *standing in the river*, which, at first, made me assume they'd taken a wrong turn on the West Highland Way and were now just quietly having a breakdown. But no. They were panning for gold. *Actual gold*. Like a Scottish version of the California gold rush, only colder and with more midges.

Gold has, of course, always been a shiny magnet for human insanity. Back in the good old days of black-and-white telly and phones you could use to brain a burglar, an ounce of the stuff cost about $65. Fast-forward to the post-pandemic years and that same ounce would set you back nearly

$3000, which explains why standing knee-deep in a freezing river suddenly looks like a viable career choice.

Just a couple of miles from where we now stood, the Cononish mine had been rediscovered like some long-lost treasure map. It was originally found decades ago but dismissed as not worth the hassle—back when gold was cheap and people still had the energy to care about things like "cost-effective extraction."

Now, however, the numbers are eye-watering. Scotgold, the company behind it—which sounds wonderfully patriotic but is actually Australian (because of course it is)—has plans to dig out half a *million* tons of ore. That's half a million tons of literal rock in the vague hope of finding 11 or 12 grams of gold per ton. The maths is, admittedly, bonkers, but it could all amount to around five tons of gold in total. And with each ton fetching upwards of £70 million, I could suddenly see the appeal of living up here with a pickaxe and a dream.

That said, gold is very, *very* heavy. I remember being handed a small piece at school once—an exciting moment that quickly lost its sparkle when our teacher revealed it was just lead. His budget didn't quite stretch to the real thing, and as he put it, buying plutonium for a demo would've involved phone calls to certain moustachioed men in bunkers. Still, it was a good lesson: gold may look small, but even a microwave-sized lump could bankrupt an entire country—or fund a small one.

And here's the kicker: you don't even need to be a massive company to strike gold. Just grab a pan and hop in the river like these beardy fellas below us. Someone even found the now-legendary *Reunion Nugget* in 2019—a three-ounce gold lump split perfectly in two like some romantic comedy plot device. Estimated value? About £80,000. Not bad for a day of splashing about in a Scottish stream and hoping no one mistakes you for a local druid.

Naturally, once that story broke, all hell broke loose. Reports emerged of actual *gangsters* descending on the area with industrial machinery and a total disregard for property rights or nature. They tore up riverbanks, trespassed across private land, and presumably kept a running playlist of 1980s action film soundtracks as they went full treasure-hunter mode.

Thankfully, the figures paddling below us didn't seem the criminal type—unless the Scottish mob has recently gone full grandad and started disguising themselves as cardigan-wearing pensioners. You never know these days.

I briefly considered whether it might be more profitable to abandon the path altogether and just walk the river all the way to Bridge of Orchy, perhaps stumbling across the legendary Reunion

Nugget's long-lost cousin. But given my track record, I'd more likely trip over a rock, sprain something crucial, and be forced to trade my water filter for a lift back to civilisation.

So, we left the glimmer of gold behind and kept climbing—backpacks slightly heavier with crushed hopes and the knowledge that we were apparently hiking over £350 million worth of hidden treasure.

The path carried us over the railway line and, along with it, any lingering hopes of discovering enough gold to retire. Instead, we now followed the ridgeline of the mountain on our right—Beinn Odhar—until we crossed back *under* the railway via a tunnel that was probably designed for sheep but repurposed for sweaty walkers. Somewhere around here we also passed a sign welcoming visitors to the national park, which was slightly confusing as we were heading *out* of the park, not into it. Apparently, they hadn't yet had the budget to sort the signs out.

This made no sense at all, because if anything, the landscape just kept levelling up. It was as if someone had been playing Scotland on ultra-hard mode and kept unlocking increasingly stunning scenery with every mile.

Beinn Odhar, looming to our right since shortly after Tyndrum, stood just shy of 3,000 feet tall, which might technically disqualify it from being a Munro, but trust me, our legs didn't care about technicalities. It had been a slog to get this far, especially with the sun blazing down on us like we owed it money. There wasn't a single cloud in the sky, and while that might sound dreamy to people not currently playing pack mule through the Highlands, it made walking feel more like slowly roasting in an outdoor sauna while wearing your entire wardrobe.

After passing under the railway line again, we found ourselves in a scenic little corridor between the train tracks and the main road. It was at this point I decided I *needed* a photo of a train going past on this utterly glorious stretch. The sort of photo that screams, "I do outdoorsy things," even if it only took 17 takes and a mild sunburn to get right.

Beyond us to the north, the landscape opened out like a Highland postcard, dominated by the towering majesty of Beinn Dorain. This is one of the most instantly recognisable mountains in Scotland, rising steeply in that 'you'll regret even thinking about climbing me' sort of way. While it looked like a beast to scale, it was also impossibly beautiful—and, rather conveniently, had already been immortalised by someone with a far better grasp of words than any of us.

That someone was Duncan Bàn Macintyre, a former gamekeeper turned poet, who composed *In Praise of Ben Doran* and generally made the rest of us look bad for not spontaneously bursting into verse every time we saw a hill.

> *Honour beyond each ben*
>
> *for Ben Doran;*
>
> *Of all I have seen beneath the sun,*
>
> *she is the most glorious for me*

He was clearly smitten. But then, who could blame him?

However, Macintyre's true moment of glory (at least in my opinion) wasn't his love letter to a mountain, but rather his biting literary takedown of a certain Archibald Fletcher of Crannach. You see, Macintyre once went off to the Battle of Falkirk as Fletcher's paid substitute, as you did in those days when war was an optional extra for rich men. But while Macintyre managed to fight the battle and come back in one piece, he had the misfortune of misplacing Fletcher's prized sword somewhere along the way. Oopsie.

Fletcher, being a man of principles and apparently no sense of irony, refused to pay Macintyre for his efforts. In response, our poetic hero didn't go back with fists—he went with verses.

He wrote a legendary poem mocking the whole farce, describing the laird's rubbish sword as little more than an overpriced butterknife, calling Fletcher an ageing badger, and highlighting the absolute shambles of his side's organisation. Despite the Jacobites technically winning the day, Macintyre made it crystal clear that Fletcher's contributions—and sword—had been utterly useless.

The poem became a hit, proving once again that revenge is a dish best served with rhyme. Fletcher, one assumes, probably regretted not handing over a couple of shillings to avoid eternal literary embarrassment.

So, with thoughts of melting in the sun, dramatic poetry, and passive-aggressive Highlanders echoing in our heads, we carried on toward Bridge of Orchy—hot, sweaty, mildly traumatised by Macintyre's wordplay, and still hoping to spot a train for that perfect Instagram moment.

Eventually, we began to make out the silhouette of what we hoped was the Bridge of Orchy Hotel, and, joy of joys, the path finally started heading downhill. This lifted our spirits immediately, which had been running on fumes. Just as we descended, a train appeared, trundling slowly along the line like it had all the time in the world. It was the first one we'd seen all day, and naturally, my vantage point was appalling, so the coveted photo opportunity was thoroughly wasted. Cheers, ScotRail.

After crossing the tracks and wobbling our way

down some unnecessarily steep steps, we followed a narrow lane into what passed for the village —which was basically a hotel, a smattering of houses, and a train station that now moonlights as a hiker's hostel. I couldn't help but imagine trying to get a decent night's kip there with freight trains screaming past your head at 3am. Cosy.

Down at the bottom of the hill, across the busy main road, we spotted some familiar faces—and not in a weird déjà vu sort of way. Our families had beaten us there and were lounging outside the hotel, sipping cold drinks and looking like they'd been enjoying civilisation a little too much.

Apparently, they hadn't seen us approaching at all—they'd *smelled* us. Or so my wife claimed. I laughed. She didn't. I think she was only half-joking.

Still, fair play to them—they had already ordered us a drink, which made the mad dash across the road feel entirely worth it, even if we did risk becoming a three-man version of Frogger in the process.

We sat and chatted for a bit, swapped stories, and I told my son about the riverside prospectors we'd seen panning for gold like it was 1849 all over again. Then, with the hotel acting as our makeshift changing room, we swapped out our crusty, sweat-drenched clothes for something a bit less... pungent. My infamous ripped trousers caused general amusement, especially with the kids, and were whisked away for proper disposal—possibly in a controlled explosion.

After an hour or so of lounging, chatting, and getting laughed at by our nearest and dearest, the ladies waved us off and headed back to Drymen and modern luxuries like showers and mattresses. We, meanwhile, refilled our water bottles using a tap outside the hotel and trudged on once more.

A short walk down through what little remained of Bridge of Orchy brought us past a scattering of bungalows, all proudly displaying "NO PARKING" signs like badges of honour. Clearly, things got competitive here when the sunshine brought out the weekend warriors.

Then we crossed the actual Bridge of Orchy and stopped in our tracks.

On the other side of the river was a campsite so perfect it looked like a brochure come to life. Flat grass. River backdrop. Firepit. Picnic benches. *Portable toilets.* It ticked every single box, including some we didn't know we had.

We all just sort of looked at each other, and without a single word, knew the decision had been made. We were staying. Sure, Inveroran was only a couple more miles away, but why push on when you've found camping Shangri-La? As my old English teacher used to say, "Education is important, but a good camping spot is more importanter."

Out came the stoves, the tent, the spiced rum, and the chilli con carne leftovers from the night before. We settled into our now well-established routine—Chris and I handled the tent, Rob played camp chef, and coffee was fortified with a splash (or three) of rum.

Only four tents were pitched here tonight, and as darkness fell and the midges emerged like tiny airborne psychopaths, we all gradually got chatting. Two girls from Aberdeen had conjured up a campfire like wilderness witches, which everyone huddled around for warmth and midge-deflection. A mother and daughter from Glasgow were roasting marshmallows and handing them out like some sort of sugary peace offering, while the last couple turned out to be from Scunthorpe—a mere stone's throw from home.

Naturally, Rob was soon deep in conversation with the entire campsite. Chris and I sat back, waiting for the inevitable: the story of how Rob met his wife, complete with height comparison visuals. You see, Rob is roughly the size of a mature giraffe, and his wife… isn't. According to their own son, if she were half an inch shorter, she'd legally qualify as a Borrower. It's their family joke. I'm just passing it on.

Eventually, the fire faded and the midges mounted a full-scale assault, so we all fled into our tents. Around 10pm, if you'd walked past the site, you'd have been forgiven for wondering why a tractor was idling loudly near the river—but no, that would just be Rob, snoring with seismic force.

I lay awake, my ears twitching at every unfamiliar noise—snoring, water rushing, the occasional involuntary fart, and something else: rustling... followed by a low grunt. Probably just a rabbit. Probably. Either way, I made a mental note that sleeping bags are absolutely useless if you ever need to run for your life. I consoled myself with another swig of rum and eventually drifted off, dreaming of stumbling across a record-breaking gold nugget, big enough to make the front page of the *Daily Mail*—and possibly pay for a hotel next time.

Bridge Of Orchy To Kinlochleven

Camping: nature's way of feeding midges.

Every camper, forever.

When I woke up, I was disappointed to discover I was still poor. No golden nuggets, no mysterious inheritance from a distant Scottish uncle, just me, my backpack, and a suspiciously sore hip. Breakfast was cooked, gear packed, and for once, we weren't the first ones off the mark. The couple from Aberdeen and the Glasgow marshmallow team had already disappeared into the morning mist, presumably with functioning knees and a renewed zest for life. The elderly duo from Scunthorpe, however, were still in blissful slumber, snoring gently in a tent that had likely witnessed more REM cycles than a Fleetwood Mac reunion.

We did a final sweep of the campsite, made sure we hadn't left any embarrassing detritus behind (like the remains of dignity or socks), dumped our rubbish in the bin provided, and set off once again, plodding up a hill and through another piney forest like we were starring in a low-budget sequel to *The Fellowship of the Ring*.

Thankfully, the day's opening climb wasn't as soul-destroying as the one before. It was more of a gentle slap to the senses—a "come on now, off you go" rather than the full Glaswegian headbutt we'd suffered 24 hours earlier. Within a mile, we broke out above the trees and were once again greeted by Highland magic: endless skies, stunning views, and a glint of Loch Tulla far off to the north, shimmering like the reward screen in a video game after a particularly harrowing level.

We rejoined the old military road, which had clearly suffered more neglect than a gym membership in February. This stretch was lumpier than a teenager's complexion, but at least it gave us the chance to walk together again rather than in single-file silence like some kind of passive-aggressive snake.

It wasn't long before we caught up with two young lads who were skipping merrily along like they were out for a stroll to the shops. They had no rucksacks, no visible gear, and no sense of the suffering they were supposed to be enduring. We assumed they were just out for the day, but no—they were walking the entire route using baggage transfers. That's right, someone else was schlepping their stuff between stops, presumably while they floated across the Highlands like smug little cherubs.

It was, admittedly, a brilliant idea, and I immediately questioned all my life choices. My back ached, my knees clicked like castanets, and the only thing I was carrying well was regret. I decided then and there that if I ever subjected myself to this madness again, I'd be paying someone else to carry my tent, and maybe even me.

The lads chatted with us for a while, during which it became clear they didn't have a map. "It's all really well signposted," one of them said with the wide-eyed innocence of someone who's never been lost in a peat bog with 3% battery and a sun that's buggered off behind a mountain. No map, no waterproofs, and probably no clue. We nodded politely and mentally prepared to call mountain rescue on their behalf sometime tomorrow.

They soon scampered ahead, leaving us to discuss their potential obituary wording. Yes, we were now fully-fledged grumpy old men muttering about "reckless youth" and "back in our day," but at least we had layers, maps, and enough Compeed to start our own pharmacy.

At the top of the hill, we were treated to a sweeping panorama of Loch Tulla and the Grampians beyond, a view that could melt even the crustiest cynic. It felt like a reward from the Highlands for still being upright and not having wandered off into a ravine.

The path, however, decided we were getting a bit too confident. What followed was a descent over the rockiest, most ankle-threatening section of military road yet. Every step was a potential hospital visit. We were so focused on foot placement we might as well have been defusing landmines—heads down, eyes glued to the rocks, missing the cinematic beauty around us because we were too busy not dying.

The path eventually eased off its vendetta, the gradient mellowed, and soon we were treated to something miraculous: tarmac. Normally the enemy of blistered feet and weary souls, this smooth strip of civilisation felt like a spa treatment by comparison. We could walk without bracing for ligament damage, and it was glorious.

We were soon at the hotel, which also offers a coffee shop during the day, so we decided to stop here in our spirit of supporting local businesses along the way. Rob and I had a coffee, while Chris just had a coke, and we took the opportunity of using the picnic benches to rest and sort our feet out.

Rob had complained of his Compeed plasters moving, so he aired his feet and applied new ones, and I did the same, as the ones I had originally put on also seemed to have moved a little. I considered just removing them, as my feet showed no signs of blisters, but then decided that this was probably only so because I had put the plasters on before I had started to walk. Chris smugly said that his feet were fine, so Rob and I growled at him intensely.

The mother and daughter from Glasgow were here, and they chatted to us for a moment, though they were clearly wary of Robin getting the family photos out again and were soon off on their way. The couple from Aberdeen were here too and looked to have settled down for the full day at their picnic bench, with all of their possessions apparently strewn around them.

We said hello, but that was as far as the conversation went, and once our feet were sorted out and our coffees had gone, we decided to move off, but not before we signed our names on the little shack at the front of the hotel.

It first looked like a small ice cream stall, but when you got closer to the shack, it was just that, and seemed to have no purpose. However, on the front was a large blackboard, along with a variety of pens, and countless people had clearly taken the opportunity to sign their name and perhaps leave a message as they passed. Most had simply left their names and the dates they had presumably passed; for instance, Robin and Kristy had passed here just the day before, but not our Robin, of course. Others had left cryptic messages such as *no surrender* or *plodding on*, which sort of made sense on a long walk such as this, but others, such as *reduce textile waste in the highlands*, did not, at least not in the context of this walk. I remembered the little accident with my trousers and wondered if others had been even more badly affected. Maybe the trail was littered with the discarded garments of semi-naked hikers, though I am sure I would have noticed if this had been the case.

We signed our names, or at least I did it on behalf of the three of us, and if you are interested, we are *The Hull Circus*, after which we moved on once again. However, a hundred yards further on, I was forced to return, as I had left both of my hiking poles next to the shack, which was not only annoying but added unwelcome distance to my day's walk. The couple who had seen us move off looked perplexed on my return but clearly realised what was happening when they saw me pass for the third time, this time carrying my sticks.

Robin subjected me to the indignity of recording my mistake on video, which was both unfair and uncalled-for, and I swore to get my revenge before the trip was out. Keep looking over your shoulder, my friend, I told him, because one day, I will be there. Of course, he would have to look down, too, in order to see me, but enough of that.

The tarmac road meandered lazily across the now pancake-flat landscape, and we did indeed pass one or two spots that looked like decent campsites. Not bad at all—but none were as good as the one we'd nabbed the night before, which reassured us that we had, for once, made the right decision. Miracles do happen.

Off to our right, in a field, a farmer was tending to his Highland cattle. I had a little chuckle when I noticed that his hair was exactly the same colour as theirs—bright, flaming red. Honestly, if he stood still too long, I reckon someone would've tried to milk him. Apparently, Scotland has the highest concentration of redheads on the planet, which is supposedly due to the fact that redheads are better at producing vitamin D. This sounds useful in a country where the sun is legally classified as a rumour.

Slight tangent, but vitamin D isn't even a vitamin. It's a hormone, which is yet another example of how everything we learned at school is a lie. Add it to the pile with Pluto being a planet and carrots helping you see in the dark.

We followed this single-track road for no more than a mile before flopping down for a quick rest at Victoria Bridge. Chris produced a bag of Haribos like he was a sugar-based magician, and we devoured the lot in record time, though he did squirrel away a few for later. Classic Chris.

The heat, by now, was more intense than yesterday's, and we were practically begging for shade. Fortunately, the path promised trees ahead, and not a moment too soon. After passing Forest Lodge and a large gate, a sign let us know we were now striding along one of Thomas Telford's Parliamentary Roads—fancy! This hopefully meant a decent surface underfoot, though at this point I'd have walked barefoot over Lego if it meant some relief from the heat.

Back in 18th-century Britain, getting anywhere was a bit of a joke. You either walked, rode a horse, or rattled around in a stagecoach like a coin in a tin, and the roads were so bad that a trip which now takes a couple of hours could take several days—assuming your wheels didn't fall off or you weren't eaten by wolves or something. The government, realising that sending messages by carrier pigeon might not cut it forever, decided to do something radical: invest in infrastructure. Enter Thomas Telford, who spent 20 years building over 900 miles of roads, around 1,000 bridges, and, for reasons known only to himself, 32 churches. Possibly just to round things up a bit.

This is particularly impressive when you consider that Telford started off as a shepherd. A literal shepherd. He taught himself stonemasonry, got into engineering, and eventually built things like the Caledonian Canal (which slices Scotland in half) and the Pontcysyllte Aqueduct in Wales— both of which are still in use, which is more than can be said for my knees. For all this, he earned the rather fabulous nickname *The Colossus of Roads*, which is probably the only pun in history worthy of a statue.

The path, as promised, was a dream. Flat, firm, and midge-free. Rob and Chris soon pulled ahead while I shuffled along at my usual "plod and contemplate mortality" pace. A little while later, I spotted them talking to two ladies, who turned out to be called Martha and Blanche, which immediately made me think we'd just wandered into an episode of *The Golden Girls*.

To my surprise, they were from Florida. Not Fort William. *Florida*. I asked if they lived here now or if they had somehow managed to dodge the ever-shifting COVID travel rules by disguising themselves as diplomats or stowing away in suitcases. They told us they had quarantined, completed multiple tests, and basically run the whole considerable gauntlet of pandemic bureaucracy to get here. I was impressed. Most people had given up trying to leave their postcode.

Blanche, who had a steely glint in her eye, told us that being in their seventies meant they couldn't afford to sit around waiting for things to get back to normal—because, frankly, they might not be around when that finally happened. I looked at her to see if she was joking. She wasn't. Dead serious.

Martha chipped in with, "None of us know when our card will get punched." Grim. But, annoyingly, also very true.

The midges were beginning to organise themselves again, like a swarm of airborne gremlins assembling for battle, so we took the hint and moved on, leaving the American ladies behind to fend for themselves. Hopefully, the going would be straightforward now—we were still on one of Telford's roads, and he had a lovely habit of designing routes that gently undulated for the benefit of horses, carts, and now, three increasingly knackered hikers.

We stopped again a short while later and had almost finished off the last of the Haribos, a solemn moment. Just as we were mourning our inevitable loss, the Floridian duo caught us up. Naturally, we offered them the last of the remaining gummy corpses, which they accepted gratefully. You've not really embraced international diplomacy until you've shared a slightly melted Tangfastic with a stranger on a Scottish moor.

I took this moment to dig deep into the murky depths of my rucksack in search of the pasta salad I'd been saving. I had big plans for this pasta salad. Gourmet visions. Sadly, I couldn't find my spork—easily one of the greatest inventions of the 20th century and absolutely vital in moments like this. With no utensil in sight, I reverted to nature's original cutlery: my hands. Or, as I prefer to call them in such situations, "the shovels God gave me." It wasn't dignified, but it was effective.

Besides, once you're classified as "hiker trash," social norms become optional.

We left the Americans once more and told them we'd see them at Kingshouse—and that it was their round. They laughed, probably assuming we were joking. We weren't. I suspected, though, that we'd never see them again at the speed they were moving, unless we took a week off and waited in the car park.

Soon after, the forest began to fall away, giving way to the endless openness of Rannoch Moor. The views were staggering—just miles of wild land, scattered lochans, and a sky that stretched out in all directions like it was trying to show off. It was down to just two elements now: land and sky. No distractions. No civilisation. No ice cream vans. Just Scotland in its rawest form.

At Ba Bridge, where the path crosses the River Ba, we caught up with the two young lads we'd met earlier. They were topping up their water, and we decided to join them for a rest. As I chatted with them, it became increasingly obvious that they were not exactly what you'd call "outdoorsy." Don't get me wrong—they were nice lads, polite and keen—but probably more used to Deliveroo than dewy hillsides. They were from Bristol, and this was their first ever trip to Scotland. I asked how they were enjoying it. "Loving it," they said.

So naturally, I decided to mess with them.

I asked if they'd seen a haggis yet. They looked confused. I explained that haggis are small, shy creatures that roam the Highlands—though few in numbers nowadays, since wolves had been reintroduced. I told them that haggis have shorter legs on one side so they can run around hills more easily. The look on their faces was absolutely priceless. I could see them trying to work it out: was I serious, or had the midges finally driven me mad?

Ba Bridge marks the halfway point between Bridge of Orchy and Kingshouse, so it's the ideal place to rest—unless you don't like being eaten alive by insects the size of pinheads. So once again, we didn't linger. It's a shame, really, because the views from there are cracking and the bridge itself is impressive. It's not entirely clear who built it—General Caulfeild or Thomas Telford—but whoever it was, they knew what they were doing. It's best seen from the river below, though unless you fancy a swim, I wouldn't recommend it.

We pressed on. The path began to tilt uphill again—not a steep incline, but the sort of long, morale-sapping gradient that lets you see exactly how far you still have to go. I stopped briefly at a small wood to adjust my rucksack, mostly because it was trying to saw my shoulders off.

As we began the long, slow climb, we naturally spread out again. Chris shot off ahead like a Labrador on espresso, I wasn't far behind for once, and Rob—true to form—brought up the rear. Uphill is not his preferred terrain.

We plodded along at our own paces, and when Chris and I reached the top, we stopped to wait for Rob. While we waited, the Bristol lads caught us up again and asked how far it was to Kingshouse. We guessed it was about two miles, though I honestly couldn't tell you whether that was accurate or just wishful thinking.

By the time Rob caught up with us, the lads were already vanishing over the brow of the hill, bouncing along like spring lambs. We, on the other hand, were already planning our next sit down.

I dropped my pack for one last breather before we tackled the long descent into the valley below. But of course, in this part of Scotland, nothing invites midges like stillness, and no sooner had I sat down than the little winged nightmares were back in formation. In about the same time it takes to mutter, "Not again," we were up and moving.

We were now solely following Telford's track, the military road having taken a loftier route over the hill—presumably for soldiers who fancied a bit of a workout. The track was empty, the views vast, and we had the whole place to ourselves.

Rounding a left-hand bend, we finally got our first proper look up towards the legendary Pass of Glencoe, a moment that felt almost cinematic. Actually, scratch that—it *was* cinematic. The area off to the right on Rannoch Moor was one of the filming locations for *Monty Python and the Holy Grail*, right after the Bridge of Death scene. If you've seen it, you'll recognise the bleak, otherworldly feel immediately. If you haven't seen it, stop reading this and sort your life out.

Following the contours of the hill, the path gradually began to slope downwards, the Glencoe Mountain Resort coming into view to our left. It was clearly doing a roaring trade, with a steady convoy of cars heading in and out like ants with coffee addictions. The resort has a café, camping and some actual toilets—luxuries by this point—but we had our hearts set on Kingshouse, another iconic waypoint on the West Highland Way.

Had I known more about the resort's recent misfortunes, I might have suggested a pit stop out of sheer sympathy. Not only were they battered by the pandemic like everyone else, but they'd also lost their main restaurant in a fire on Christmas Day 2019. Santa really dropped the ball on that one. The place had been closed and thankfully nobody was hurt, but it was still a devastating blow to their business. They've been trying to bounce back ever since, and I reckon anyone passing through who fancies a brew and a bacon bap should pop in and throw some money their way.

We carried on, passing the striking Blackrock Cottage—a whitewashed wonder that's probably one of the most photographed buildings in the entire Highlands. I took my own obligatory snap, naturally, and imagined how peaceful it must be to stay there. Unfortunately, it's owned by the Ladies Scottish Climbing Club, meaning it's both off-limits to us mere mortals *and* a no-go zone for those of us not blessed with the right chromosome configuration. So, with a collective sigh of rejection, we trudged on toward Kingshouse, which was now tantalisingly close—less than a mile to go.

Just before reaching the road, we spotted the two young lads we'd met earlier, now slumped dramatically on the verge like extras in a war film. One of them, looking like a man who had recently lost all hope, asked us if we knew where the nearest place to get water was. Rob, Chris and I exchanged a look that said, *Really?* and told them that Kingshouse was just down the road and had water, coffee, and probably a defibrillator if needed.

At that point, one of the lads suddenly leapt up like a man possessed and sprinted towards Kingshouse clutching two empty bottles, arms flailing, legs wobbling. We tried to explain that the path went straight there anyway and that he was essentially just running in the correct direction *but* with added panic. Either he didn't hear us or decided hydration was more urgent than logic, so off he went, and we followed at a far more sensible pace.

The Kingshouse Hotel is a proper West Highland Way institution. It offers rooms, beer, and shelter from the elements—plus, just across the charming little River Etive, a decent wild camping spot for tight-fisted romantics like us. But what it's really famous for is the red deer. Most evenings, the deer wander right up to the hotel like a pack of furry freeloaders, entirely unbothered by smelly, weary hikers cluttering up the car park.

When I'd looked at the hotel's website before the trip, I'd spotted a politely worded notice asking guests *not* to feed the deer chocolate, crisps or Mars Bars. A sentence that's both very specific and extremely telling. I mean, really—what kind of tourist looks at a majestic Scottish stag and thinks, *You know what you need, mate? A Snickers.*

It gets worse. Not the walking — the tourists. Kingshouse is notorious for traffic queues caused by people stopping in the middle of the road, doors flung open, hazard lights blinking, all so they can creep up on a red deer and take a blurry selfie while muttering "Oh wow" in six different accents.

Apparently, a particularly large stag once charged after a tourist who tried to offer it a chocolate digestive. We assume he was more of a Jammie Dodger kind of guy. But even that pales in comparison to the drunken soul who, at 5am, attempted to get a deer to drink whisky. True story. Stag do, indeed.

Now, I shouldn't have to say this, but if you ever find yourself face-to-antler with a wild, unpredictable, and potentially quite stabby animal in the small hours of the morning, don't try to get it drunk. Especially not with whisky. And *definitely* not with whiskey — that's Irish. Scottish deer are very particular about their vowels.

In all seriousness, the sight of deer quietly grazing around Kingshouse must be utterly majestic — if you can resist throwing crisps at them or trying to get one to pose for your Insta story. So you can imagine my excitement when I spotted one near the main building... only to realise it wasn't moving. Nor was it real. Still, 10/10 for craftsmanship.

We rolled into the beer garden with high hopes for a sit-down and a pint, but alas, every picnic bench was already taken by the freshly-laundered and suspiciously clean. I doubted many of them had just walked twelve miles through the mountains. Most looked like they'd just hopped off the coach parked next to the building, possibly after being told the deer would be signing autographs later.

Rob suggested we sit on the stone wall nearby, but it was right next to a bin that was apparently hosting a buzzing insect rave, so we went inside instead.

The interior was blessedly cool and, strangely, almost empty. One friendly chap told us not to get too excited — they were basically out of food. Not ideal, but Chris wandered off anyway to see what scraps remained. Ten minutes later, he reappeared with what can only be described as a hiker's fever dream: a pint of beer and an ice cream for each of us.

I'm not sure what your dietitian would say, but to me, that is the definition of a balanced meal. Hot day, tired legs, mild dehydration... yes, I think beer and dairy is the perfect recovery combo. Take that, sports science.

The ice cream hit first — cold, sweet and gone in seconds. Then the beer followed, lighting up the brain in a slightly giddy way. Beer on an empty stomach is like rocket fuel, and soon we were laughing too loud and beginning to attract the kind of attention that usually results in the phrase "I think it's time you left now."

Before heading off, we decided to use the toilets, and this is where things began to unravel. Rob went first, followed by Chris, and I stayed behind to guard our rucksacks, just in case anyone had a thing for sweaty nylon sacks that smelled of desperation and crushed Haribo.

When Rob returned, I went in — only to nearly collapse from shock as Chris leapt out from behind the door like a deranged jack-in-the-box. I told him, politely but firmly, to wait outside and stop trying to kill me. Once finished, I rejoined him and had an idea.

"Film me playing the piano," I said.

Chris gave me a look. "You can play the piano?"

"There's a lot you don't know about me," I replied mysteriously.

He started filming. I sat down at the hotel lobby's upright piano, composed myself like a true maestro, and solemnly announced to the camera, "Beethoven's Fifth, in C Minor."

Then I absolutely *battered* that poor piano. The noise that erupted could only be described as catastrophic — like someone had rolled a bag of spanners down an escalator. Notes clashed. Octaves wept. Somewhere, Beethoven spun in his grave like a jet engine.

As Chris choked with laughter and told me that no, I absolutely could *not* play piano, we scarpered back into the bar, grabbed our rucksacks and prepared for a swift exit before security could locate us.

As we made our getaway, I noticed a young German lady sat quietly in the corner. I smiled, greeted her, and introduced her to my two *Scheißkopf* friends. For those unfamiliar with German, that's "sh*thead" — a term of great affection when used correctly, and much less offensive in its native tongue. Honest.

She chuckled, which I took as approval, and having now exhausted my high school German, we waved goodbye, slung our packs back on our aching shoulders, and marched back into the wilds once more.

We crossed the bridge over the River Etive and immediately swung left, rejoining the old military road like the obedient little backpack-toting masochists we are. From here, the route played a familiar tune—hugging the side of a mountain while keeping a flirty eye on the main road. Sometimes we were right next to it, sometimes perched high above, like smug vultures watching the lorries thunder past below.

One of those lorries, clearly driven by someone who thought they were being hilarious, let rip with a horn blast that nearly sent me to an early grave. I was so startled I very nearly needed a change of trousers—which, given the history of my trousers on this walk, would've just been another tragic chapter in a long-running saga of fabric-based misfortune.

To our right, across the road, loomed Buachaille Etive Mòr, looking every inch the cover star of a Scotland calendar and entirely oblivious to the fact that it had once played a starring role in Hitchcock's *The 39 Steps*. A little further along was Buachaille Etive Beag, which got its own cinematic moment in *Highlander*, specifically the opening battle scene that was equal parts epic and utterly confusing. Still, Sean Connery swinging a sword in a kilt? Iconic. If it's good enough for immortal sword-fighting lunatics, it's good enough for us.

As we stomped along, I noticed that I'd managed to cut my finger—presumably while thrashing that poor piano back at Kingshouse like I was trying to summon Beethoven from the grave. I didn't bother with a plaster; it had mostly stopped bleeding, and anyway, I deserved a small injury for acting like a six-year-old with a sugar rush and no musical ability whatsoever.

The walk to the foot of the Devil's Staircase turned out to be a full three miles—two more than I had optimistically guessed, but who's counting? (Answer: me. Always.) At the bottom, we flopped onto a patch of grass to take a break and snap a few photos. A nearby lay-by was buzzing with tourists, all of whom were making the brave ascent to... the nearest photo op.

We watched with great amusement as one bloke emerged from his car, opened the boot, took out a massive red rucksack, slung it over one shoulder, posed next to the sign for a dramatic "Look at me, I'm so rugged" photo, then promptly dumped the bag back in the car and drove off. I mean... commitment to the bit, sure, but also, what?

I turned to Rob and Chris, expecting to share

the joy of having witnessed peak tourist nonsense, but of course they hadn't been paying attention. Too busy tying shoelaces or inspecting the inside of their eyelids or whatever it is they do when comedy gold is happening right in front of them.

Still chuckling to myself, we hoisted our own bags (which were *not* props, thank you very much) and turned our faces toward the Devil's Staircase.

"I've heard it's not as bad as people say," I told the lads.

And just like that, I tempted fate.

The Devil's Staircase didn't get its name from a jolly local who liked a dramatic flair for cartography. No, legend has it that either General Wade's poor road-building lads dubbed it after crawling up here one too many times with sore feet and existential despair—or it was the dam builders from nearby Blackwater who gave it the name, after watching their mates fail to return from a pub night and concluding, quite reasonably, that they'd been dragged off by Satan himself. Frankly, I could see it. You only had to look at the slope to realise this place had "hellish" written all over it.

We started the climb with the grim optimism of condemned men, agreeing to reconvene at the top—*if* we made it. Chris, once again fuelled by rocket fuel or possibly Haribo, shot up the thing like a mountain goat with something to prove. I took a few dozen steps and already felt like I'd aged a decade. Meanwhile, Rob remained motionless at the bottom, possibly trying to negotiate terms with gravity before committing to the incline.

It was an unrelenting slog. The summit sits at just over 1,800 feet, the highest point on the West Highland Way, which is great if you like achievements and not so great if you enjoy oxygen and functioning knees. It took me almost an hour of steady, wheezing effort. Halfway up, I encountered a lady descending and asked if she wouldn't mind passing a message to the bald bloke lagging behind: tell him to pull his finger out before the devil nabs him next.

By the time I arrived at the top, Chris was already horizontal, sipping water and offering sweets like some benevolent trail fairy. I gratefully accepted—anything to stop my lungs sounding like a distressed accordion. With no sign of Rob, I got the drone out for a quick aerial scan, partly to admire the view and partly to check he hadn't collapsed into a heather bush. We found him soon enough, mid-conversation with the same lady, and when he noticed the drone, he saluted it in true Rob fashion—two fingers, full sass.

Eventually, he arrived, gasping, red-faced, and muttering dark things about stairs and death. Chris rewarded him with sweets too, probably as a kind of peace offering. We rested a little longer, but the day wasn't getting any younger, so we heaved the rucksacks back on and headed into the jaws of the mountains ahead.

We got a little excited over a distant, looming peak and debated whether it might be Ben Nevis. Given the rare gift of clear skies, it wasn't out of the question, though none of us were willing to bet more than a fruit pastille on it.

What came next was blessedly easier. The route levelled out, then gently dipped and bobbed as we descended. Kinlochleven beckoned with promises of greasy chips and foamy pints, and with every step downhill, we felt closer to salvation.

Looking back, we had magnificent views over the Blackwater Reservoir, its water level worryingly low but still photogenically dramatic. The dam itself is the longest in Scotland—almost a kilometre long—and you can just about make it out if you squint in the right direction. Built entirely with hand tools (because health and safety wasn't invented yet), it was one of the last major construction projects to rely on the legendary navvies—those hard-as-nails blokes who built half the country with nothing but shovels, muscle and a complete disregard for personal well-being.

Water from the reservoir rushes down through a series of pipes to Kinlochleven below, where turbines spin it into electricity—originally to power an aluminium smelter, though that's long gone now. Still, it's impressive. A whole dam built with nothing but elbow grease, curses, and probably a few dozen whisky bottles. Makes you feel a bit guilty for grumbling about your backpack. Almost.

We were back on the old military road, although at this point it was barely more than a suggestion of a path—less a road and more of a vague hint in the undergrowth. Still, as we dragged ourselves onward, it widened slowly, as if sensing that we were at the very limits of our patience and knees. Eventually, we emerged onto what looked suspiciously like a logging road—wide, smooth, and utterly vertical.

Chris and I were out front, not through speed or fitness, but simply due to a complete refusal to stop. Robin, however, was somewhere in the distant past. We did glance back at one point and briefly considered waiting for him, but ultimately decided he was probably still alive and definitely not our responsibility.

By now, the only thing on our minds was finding somewhere—*anywhere*—to camp. We would've settled for a vaguely horizontal patch of dirt and a breeze strong enough to deter midges, but no such paradise presented itself. The path grew steeper with every turn, tricking us repeatedly into thinking we'd reached the valley floor. But no—just another corner, another drop, another moment to question all of our life choices.

Eventually, we found ourselves walking alongside the enormous pipelines that carry water down from the Blackwater Dam. They weren't exactly scenic, but they did suggest we were nearing civilisation. We even bumped into a group of ladies out on a walk, though one of them appeared to be hiking in *flip-flops*. I mean, I've seen some questionable footwear on the trail, but this looked like a bold new strategy in podiatric warfare. We asked how far it was to the village, but no one knew. Classic.

Finally, we stumbled across a bridge over the River Leven and limped into the very outskirts of Kinlochleven. A pristine patch of grass teased us with its flat, soft welcome... and a massive 'No Camping' sign. So that was a no, then.

Luckily, just around the corner, we struck gold —an actual dedicated campsite, complete with showers, toilets, a shop, laundry, a washing-up room, and, most glorious of all, glamping pods. Glamping. Pods. Beds, roofs, walls—civilisation! Chris looked at me. I looked at Chris. No words needed: *get the pod.*

We dumped our packs and staggered into the office like survivors of a shipwreck, only to find... nothing. No staff. No one. Just a little sign announcing, with cruel finality, that reception had closed at 6pm. It was now 6:07. I stared at the clock as if willing time to reverse through sheer rage. Seven. Bloody. Minutes. We had missed salvation by the time it takes to make a Pot Noodle.

Crestfallen, we shuffled off to the tent area and debated whether to go back and find Robin. After a short pause to reflect, we concluded that the kindest thing we could do was get the tent up so he'd have somewhere to collapse when he eventually made it. That's real friendship, that is —constructing shelter instead of hiking back up a sadistic slope to rescue a man who made his own choices.

We pitched the tent with military efficiency. I'd say it was teamwork, but mostly it was panic —the sun always seems to set *three times faster* when you're putting up a tent, and the midges had already declared war.

And then, just as the final peg was hammered in and we were silently debating if we had the strength to eat, a shadow appeared along the path: Robin. Dishevelled, sweaty, limping, and utterly broken. He reached us, collapsed like a tranquilised rhino, and groaned something unintelligible that might have been gratitude or just the sound of his soul leaving his body.

We all sat in silence for a blessed minute... and then the midges arrived.

With a mutual grunt of horror, we leapt into action, driven by the kind of urgency usually reserved for fire drills and bear attacks. First priority: cram every item we owned into the tent before it became a blood buffet. Second priority: disappear—into the tent, into the night, into whatever corner of our souls hadn't yet been eaten alive.

This had been a long day. A *very* long day. But we were one day closer to the end. And only one apocalypse away from needing new blood.

We wandered into town—if you could call a handful of buildings and a chip shop a "town"— crossing yet another bridge that gave us front-row seats to a dramatic torrent of water doing its best impression of a raging mountain river. It was impressive, sure, but our first port of call was the chip shop, followed closely by the pub next door. Support local, eat chips, drink beer: the hiker's code.

Inside the chip shop, a young lady with the commanding presence of a Roman general was running the show. She insisted we all wear face masks, which we happily did—less out of public health concern and more to slow the midges down. As she cooked our food, she barked orders at her poor assistant, who appeared to be doing his best to vanish into the fryer. Her expression was what I can only describe as onion-destroying. She'll go far in life, I thought, and hopefully far away.

Waiting for the food felt like watching paint dry in a sauna full of midges. I'd ordered first, naturally, which meant I got served last—because logic. Rob managed to bag us a bench in the sun, which still blazed in the evening sky, thanks to us being about 900 miles north of anywhere sensible. We sat down to eat and promptly became a buffet for every winged parasite in the county.

Incorporating several midges into my meal for that extra protein hit, I cracked and retreated beneath my fleece—a decision I regretted almost instantly. It was effective at keeping the midges out but came with the minor drawback of turning me into a human pressure cooker. Chris sensibly opted to eat while walking, which at least kept the bugs slightly off balance. I joined him, inhaling my food like a Dyson on full power.

Bellies full and dignity mostly intact, we legged it to the Tailrace Inn like men fleeing an invisible plague—which, to be fair, we were.

Inside, the place was packed. Scotland were about to kick off against Denmark, and the pub was vibrating with the collective hopes of half a nation. All the tables were reserved, but the landlady clearly took pity on our bedraggled, midge-bitten faces and found us a spot right in the middle of the action.

As we pondered our pints, we proudly mentioned that we'd done a few extra miles today to make tomorrow's final stretch just 13 miles. She looked at us as if we'd just said the moon was made of Irn-Bru. "It's 16 miles to Fort William," she said flatly. "They changed the finishing point. The guidebooks haven't caught up yet."

Our smiles slowly deflated like a sad balloon at a disappointing party. We stared at her, hoping this was some kind of elaborate Scottish wind-up. It wasn't. Sixteen miles. Brilliant.

We took our pints and slumped into our seats like deflated soufflés. The football was already on, and the pub was alive with Scottish pride. We joined in by cheering enthusiastically... when Denmark scored.

Big mistake.

Three English blokes, leaping up and celebrating Denmark's goal in the middle of a pub full of Scots, is not a recommended life choice. Dozens of heads swivelled in unison, like owls with anger issues. We smiled weakly and sat down.

Then Denmark scored again. And like complete morons, we did it *again*.

More death stares. More shrinking into seats. We briefly considered hiding under the table or faking a sudden illness. Thankfully, Denmark didn't score a third. Possibly because the wrath of the pub would've torn a hole in the fabric of time.

At 8pm, with the crowd now glued to the match and us temporarily invisible, we made our escape through the back like criminal masterminds. Only,

I'd left my fleece. Of course I had.

I crept back in like Gollum retrieving his precious, expecting a volley of abuse. But no one noticed. The fleece was still there, and I made a hasty second exit, clutching it like it had just come off the catwalk at Milan.

Back to the campsite we went, battling a cloud of midges every step of the way. With no campfires allowed, there was only one solution left: hide. We used the facilities, dived into the tent like SAS soldiers escaping under cover of night, and that was that.

I don't even remember going to sleep. No dreams, no final thoughts—just immediate unconsciousness, the kind you earn after a long day, a long walk, and possibly offending an entire pub full of Scottish football fans.

Kinlochleven To Fort William

Too much fresh air is not a thing.
Me

Someone, in a fit of insanity, had set the alarm for 5.30am. After fumbling to locate the source of the infernal beeping and contemplating whether murder before sunrise was justifiable, I remembered it was my alarm. I had set it. On purpose. For reasons.

We'd agreed to get up *especially* early so we could hit the trail at first light, thanks to the extra miles we now had to cover. This meant dragging ourselves from our tents at a time when even the midges were still rubbing the sleep out of their evil little eyes.

We'd told the girls we'd meet them in Fort William around mid-afternoon. That was the goal. Why? Because we'd booked ourselves a celebratory meal at the Clachan back in Drymen to mark the completion of this grand, blister-inducing folly—*if* we actually made it, of course. No pressure.

The thinking was that if we finished by mid-afternoon, we'd have enough time to drive back, decontaminate ourselves with a proper shower, and attempt to appear vaguely human in a restaurant. A tall order. While we'd each brought wipes and attempted various dubious methods of trail-side hygiene, there's a certain point at which you stop masking the smell and just try to stay downwind of civilisation.

By six o'clock sharp—or a minute before, to be precise—we had packed up our tents and sleeping bags and were already on the move, crunching our way out of Kinlochleven with all the subtlety of a stampeding gravel elephant. If you were staying at the campsite and got woken up that morning… you're welcome. Nothing says "good morning" like the thunderous trudge of three crusty hikers sounding like a bag of spanners being dragged across a quarry.

We passed the skeletal remains of the old aluminium smelter, which, back in the day, had actually been the reason Kinlochleven existed at all. These days, it's home to a giant indoor climbing centre complete with a refrigerated wall, because apparently some people aren't content with hiking over Scotland's mountains—they want to simulate Everest in a tin shed too. The centre nearly didn't survive, having caught fire not long ago and being rebuilt shortly afterwards, though wisely without the sauna, which had been fingered as the likely firestarter. Somewhere in that building is a small museum called *The Aluminium Story*, which I can only assume is used to put insomniacs out of their misery. There's also a microbrewery attached, which sounds considerably more worth visiting. Priorities, and all that.

Other than that, Kinlochleven doesn't have much else to shout about. I checked the local library's website once, and it proudly boasted "books" as one of its main attractions. Honestly.

With all that inspiration, we decided it was definitely time to leave.

The village was more or less deserted as we shuffled through its silent, sodium-lit streets. Dawn was just beginning to leak in from the east, and the only sign of life we encountered was a reluctant-looking dog being walked by a very enthusiastic owner. The poor thing was clearly not a morning hound—it gave us a baleful look and spent most of its walk trying to eat something unidentifiable off the pavement. A relatable mood, really.

Just before we left town for good, we passed a front garden that contained what can only be described as an infestation of garden gnomes. Hundreds of them. Possibly thousands. It was like Snow White had opened a time-share village for short porcelain sociopaths. Naturally, our own pint-sized friend Chris leapt the fence and posed for a photo with his bearded kin.

Unfortunately, the gnome-hugging antics set off someone's dog, which proceeded to bark like it had just seen a burglar made entirely out of sausages. Lights snapped on in the upstairs windows, and without so much as a goodbye to Chris's new family, we legged it out of Kinlochleven like a group of naughty schoolboys caught nicking apples.

We didn't look back. Mostly because we were too knackered. But also because I'm not sure we'd have been able to resist stealing a gnome.

We'd planned to make a quick detour to see the Grey Mare's Tail—a spectacular 150-foot cascade that throws itself into the valley with all the dramatic flair of a soap opera exit—but with the extra miles we now had to cover, we reluctantly scrapped the idea. Later, I discovered that it was actually just a short hop from the car park by St Paul's Church, and we probably could've managed it with time to spare. Cue the regret. I vowed to come back one day and give it the attention it clearly deserved. I mean, it's a waterfall carved by glaciers during the last ice age—what's not to love?

Back in the 17th century, this area was used as a lookout post by the Covenanters—early Scottish Nationalists who hid in the hills and glared menacingly towards any government troops on the horizon (read: English). The spot offered excellent views of the valley and, presumably, decent midge exposure.

Scottish nationalism, of course, has a long and storied past. Sometimes glorious, sometimes messy, and often accompanied by bagpipes and shouting. While the movement is largely peaceful these days, one of the more impressive incidents in its rebellious résumé happened in 1950, when a group of Glaswegian students sauntered into Westminster Abbey and *removed* the Stone of Scone. Whether they stole it or liberated it depends entirely on your politics and whether or not your granny waves a Saltire.

The Stone of Scone—or, as it should definitely be called, *The Stone of Destiny*—was historically used to crown the Kings of Scotland. The last to get the royal bottom treatment was John Balliol in 1292. You might remember him as the puppet king Edward I stuck on the Scottish throne, much to the fury of Robert the Bruce, who wasn't really the "let's share power" type.

When Edward Longshanks (yes, the Hammer of the Scots) invaded in 1296, he did what all good invaders do—looted everything shiny. This included the Stone of Scone, which he carted off to Westminster Abbey. There, he had a special throne made to house it, as a big "ha-ha" to the Scots and a visual way of saying, "You're mine now."

Fast forward to Christmas Day, 1950, when Ian

Hamilton, Gavin Vernon, Kay Matheson and Alan Stuart somehow pulled off the heist of the century. And when I say "somehow," I mean that in the same way you might marvel at a cat managing to dial 999—there was more luck than judgement involved. On their first go, they got caught by a night watchman and booted out. On the second try, they *broke the stone in half*. Because of course they did.

Dragging 150kg of sacred rock on a coat and stuffing it into a Ford Anglia (a car about the size of an average handbag) is no mean feat. They almost wrecked the suspension. A passing policeman even chatted to them—but since the break-in hadn't been discovered yet, they got away scot-free. Pun very much intended.

Instead of legging it straight back to Scotland like anyone with half a brain might do, they doubled down on cunning and hid the stone in a Kent field. Meanwhile, the authorities absolutely lost it. The border between England and Scotland was shut—something that hadn't happened in about four centuries—and there was more panic than when someone whispers "out of Irn-Bru" in a Glasgow corner shop.

Eventually, in 1951, the Stone was found in Arbroath Abbey and returned to Westminster. All four culprits were questioned, but no charges were brought. The government decided prosecuting them might only stoke the flames of nationalism, which at the time was more smouldering peat than roaring bonfire. And if any of this sounds familiar, it may be because it was turned into a film in 2008 called *The Stone of Destiny*, which is well worth a watch if you enjoy tales of historical burglary, student mischief, and mild diplomatic chaos.

Of course, not all expressions of Scottish nationalism have been so delightfully whimsical. Enter the Scottish National Liberation Army (SNLA), a fringe terrorist group whose résumé includes sending letter bombs to the Princess of Wales, attempting to poison water supplies, and sending caustic soda disguised as massage oil to Cherie Blair. Classy bunch.

They also claimed responsibility for train derailments and bomb threats at oil companies —just your average day in the office for this lot. They even criticised the Scottish National Party itself, accusing the SNP of clinging to their comfy government jobs and never actually wanting independence because, well, what would they do after that? The SNLA's political wing, the Scottish Freedom Party, does exist online—mainly on Facebook and Twitter—where they enjoy the dizzying support of about 15 followers. To put it in perspective, that's fewer than the number of people still watching *Neighbours*.

And finally, in perhaps the most Scottish fact of all: the national animal of Scotland is the unicorn.

No, really. It's not a lion, not a stag, not even an angry bagpipe. A unicorn. It's meant to represent purity, strength, and wild independence—oh, and legend has it that it's the *only* creature that can defeat a lion. Which, conveniently, is the national animal of England. Subtle, Scotland. Very subtle.

But hey, unicorns are fiercely proud, elusive, and impossible to control. If that doesn't sound like Scotland, I don't know what does.

We moved on, leaving Kinlochleven and Scottish politics behind us—for now at least—and, in classic West Highland Way fashion, were immediately met with a hill that looked like it had personal beef with our thighs. A steep forest track loomed in front of us like some kind of leafy punishment, and as we entered the woods, we found ourselves plunged into a gloom so thick it felt like walking into a wardrobe. The faint daylight that had just about lit up the village was now thoroughly blocked by a solid wall of pine, making the uphill slog feel like a very early morning game of blindfolded mountaineering.

Trudging uphill, dodging roots, rocks and regret, and crossing one or two murmuring streams, we finally burst out onto the side of a mountain and were greeted by a breathtaking panorama—assuming we could still breathe. The view back down to Kinlochleven was something else, as were the heavy clouds draped over the surrounding peaks like a bad omen. We were about to walk straight into them, of course, because apparently we'd offended the weather gods at some point. Still, one silver lining to this rapidly greying sky was the magnificent view to the west: Loch Leven, calmly glinting below like it didn't have a care in the world.

Now, Loch Leven is a sea loch—meaning it's connected to the ocean at Ballachulish, in case you were wondering what made it salty and smug. While we couldn't see it from where we stood, somewhere at the far end of that loch sits a little island called Eilean Munde. Sounds lovely, doesn't it? Idyllic. Except no one lives there. It's not a holiday hotspot. It's a graveyard. Specifically, it's the burial ground for the Clan Macdonald of Glencoe, whose legacy is mostly known for being absolutely shafted on one of the most infamous nights in Scottish history.

Yes, we're talking about the Glencoe Massacre —Friday the 13th of February, 1692. An actual Friday the 13th, just to really hammer the point home. The Campbells of Argyll turned up at the Macdonalds' door asking for shelter, and, in accordance with ancient Highland hospitality, the Macdonalds took them in. Fed them. Housed them. Probably made them a nice cuppa. What they didn't realise was that the Campbells had come armed with more than just bad attitudes. They had royal orders to slaughter every Macdonald male under the age of seventy while they slept—an instruction so appallingly dishonourable that even some of the Campbells were said to be outraged.

Betrayal under trust was seen as a cardinal sin back then, and rightly so. It wasn't even about the number of deaths—it was about the sheer snivelling cowardice of it all. It was the kind of move that gets you booed off the stage at Highland history re-enactments. That said, not all Campbells were in on it. There are tales of a few breaking their swords rather than following through with the order, and one or two even tried to warn the Macdonalds. Sadly, it wasn't enough.

The massacre wasn't random, either. The Macdonalds were seen as a bit of a nuisance—constantly in trouble with the law and locked in a long-standing feud with the Campbells. They were also a little slow in pledging loyalty to the shiny new monarchs, William and Mary, which made them prime candidates for an "example." A very stabby, dishonourable, sleeping-bag-of-death example.

And if you're wondering whether that grudge is still alive today—oh, it absolutely is. The Clachaig Inn, not far from Glencoe, still has a sign on its door that reads "No hawkers or Campbells," which may or may not be a joke, depending on who you ask and how many whiskies they've had.

Oh, and speaking of cinematic drama—just behind that very same inn is where they built

Hagrid's hut for the *Harry Potter* films, complete with pumpkin patch. And while we're at it, *Skyfall Lodge*, the fictional home of James Bond, was supposedly up here too. Although let's not ruin it by pointing out the actual house was built in leafy Surrey. Movie magic, eh?

But forget fiction—when it comes to backstabbing, betrayal, and dramatic mountaintop locations, Scotland's history has got Hollywood beat hands down.

It was time to move on, although we did pause briefly to admire the view—well, what little there was of it. Thick clouds still swirled around the mountains like a fog machine on full blast at a haunted house disco, and I couldn't help but wonder what spectacular sights we were missing. I'd heard that some of the best views of the entire West Highland Way were along this stretch. Naturally, the Scottish weather had decided to give us its finest curtain of grey instead. Classic.

Still, the Old Military Road was guiding us once again, and as usual, it had the decency to be relatively easy underfoot. But while the path was cooperating, my legs most definitely weren't. Rob and Chris had somehow launched themselves forward like caffeinated mountain goats, and the distance between us grew faster than my will to live. I wondered if they were speeding up or if I was slowing down, and after some scientific pondering, concluded that yes, I was indeed just crap.

Eventually, they did stop to wait for me—probably more out of pity than camaraderie—and we shared some Kendal Mint Cake, which gave me a brief sugar-fuelled illusion that I could conquer Everest. That lasted about thirty steps. Soon enough, I was flagging again like a knackered Labrador on a very hot day.

After a long, slow plod through the murk, I found the lads waiting for me at the ruins of an old cottage—one I recognised from countless photos, because apparently even derelict stone walls can become Instagram-famous these days. It's something of a minor celebrity along the West Highland Way, and I was pleased to finally meet it in person.

Rob and Chris had apparently decided that I needed food before I collapsed dramatically on the track and started begging passing hikers for Kendal Mint Cake handouts. I agreed wholeheartedly. Usually, we'd had at least a nibble before setting off each day, but not today—and the result was a walking corpse powered only by sarcasm and spite. One of my closest friends once described my entire life as "a series of awkward and humiliating moments separated by snacks," and to be honest, I'm not going to argue.

In his usual no-nonsense fashion, Rob whipped up a hot meal and a coffee on the stove, and within minutes we were all sitting on rocks like some weird outdoor brunch club, finally warming up for the first time all day. It was the first time all week, in fact, that we had felt genuinely cold. We looked around and realised something else too: we hadn't seen another human being since leaving Kinlochleven that morning. Just us, the wind, and the faint smell of instant coffee.

The ruined building was more substantial than I expected, with a jagged chimney jutting out of the remains like it had a point to prove. Despite the years, the weather, and whatever sheep-based incidents had occurred nearby, that chimney was still standing, flipping the bird to the elements.

Cottages like this are scattered across the highlands, and many of them have the same grim backstory: the Highland Clearances. From the mid-1700s, landlords realised they could make more money if they booted out the tenant farmers who'd been scratching out a living for generations and replaced them with sheep, who presumably didn't complain as much or ask for housing. The evicted families were shoved into crofting communities, expected to go kelp-picking or fishing instead of farming, and were understandably furious about this downgrade in both job satisfaction and dignity.

Some landlords even paid for their evictees to sail off to America or Australia—possibly out of guilt, or more likely just to make sure they were well and truly someone else's problem. Then, in the mid-1800s, the Highland Potato Famine swept through and finished off what little hope was left. The result? A once-bustling landscape now littered with silent, crumbling cottages and the ghosts of communities that were never meant to vanish.

With the cold beginning to creep through our jackets, we decided it was time to get moving again. I have to admit, the food had worked wonders, and suddenly I felt like a new man—or at least a slightly less broken one. For the first time in days, I was not only keeping up with Rob and Chris... I was ahead of them. Admittedly only for a short while, and probably because they let me, but still—I was taking the lead, and it felt bloody marvellous.

We'd been steadily heading west for a while, but now the path arced northward, hugging the contours of the mountains like a lost puppy looking for affection. Ahead, forests came into view—finally, a change of scenery, though they weren't exactly the whispering, ancient kind from fantasy novels. These were working forests, and large sections had been clear-felled. Not pretty, admittedly, but I'm pragmatic about these things. If you're reading the paperback version of this book, then congratulations—you're part of the reason the view looks like it's been attacked by a chainsaw-wielding maniac—as am I.

There are upsides, though. Ground-nesting

birds apparently love these clear-felled sites, something I found out personally when a grouse launched itself out of the heather like a feathery grenade, nearly giving me a heart attack and probably shaving a year off my life expectancy. The remaining stumps help prevent soil erosion, and the logging's done in patches, with plenty of forest left surrounding them. So yes, it looks a bit rough, but it's not all doom and gloom—unless you're the tree, obviously.

It still wasn't warming up. Heavy cloud lingered over the high ground, and I stopped to pull my fleece on, eyeing the sky like it had personally insulted me. The air had that *I'm-thinking-about-raining-but-might-just-tease-you* quality, so I left the waterproofs in the bag but shoved them right at the top, just in case Mother Nature decided to stop faffing about and get on with it.

I'd managed to get ahead of Rob and Chris for once and was striding along the forest tracks alone when I bumped into Duncan. Duncan was out on his bike, doing a circuit of Ben Nevis—because of course he was—and had stopped to tinker with his chain. I thought this might be a quick "morning, nice bike, lovely weather" kind of encounter. It was not. Duncan, it turns out, had stories. Lots of stories. And opinions. And unsolicited facts about gear ratios. I'd apparently encountered a one-man podcast.

By the time Robin and Chris caught up, I'd been

nodding along for so long I started to worry I was developing whiplash. Duncan wasn't *boring*, exactly—just... enthusiastically relentless. I'd only had to slap myself across the face once or twice to stay awake, which is practically a social win. His hair was impressive, though. I've never seen follicles so determined to evacuate through the nostrils. I'd been moments away from using the old "LOOK, A DISTRACTION!" routine and legging it while he was turned around, but thankfully, my trusty companions had arrived.

Or so I thought. Instead, they clocked the situation instantly, smirked like a pair of teenage delinquents, and coolly walked past me without even making eye contact. Honestly, if betrayal had a sound, it would be the crunch of their boots ignoring my plight. I grimaced, made my excuses ("must dash, I've got some important trudging to do"), and finally escaped after two more minutes of polite wriggling.

We pressed on through what felt like the world's longest woodland, broken only by an information board that Chris and Rob had stopped to inspect. It told us about the Battle of Inverlochy—or, more precisely, about the Macdonalds chasing down the Campbells afterwards in a sort of 17th-century highland Benny Hill sketch.

The battle happened in February 1645, a time when Scotland decided it fancied a bit of the English Civil War chaos and jumped into the fray.

Irish troops joined in too—because why not?—and after all the usual allegiances and betrayals, the Campbells ended up backing the wrong side and getting spectacularly wrecked for their trouble.

The real highlight of the sign, though, wasn't the history—it was the graffiti. Scrawled in the top-left corner in permanent black marker (recently applied, judging by the sharpie boldness) were the words: *"never trust a MacDonald or a MacLeod, murderous, traitorous scum."* Their words, not mine. Maybe the grudge really does live on. Who knew the West Highland Way was also a passive-aggressive historical feud trail?

And for the record, Inverlochy—the battle's actual location—is about five miles north, so why this sign was here, in the middle of absolutely nowhere, remains a mystery. But then again, nothing says "welcome to the Highlands" like a random bit of civil war rage in the woods.

The woods came and went like they were on a rotating stage set, and just when we thought we might be heading downhill for good, the path took a smug little upward lurch at a site overlooking a loch to the west. Naturally, there was another information board—Scotland's favourite form of entertainment—and this one was a corker. It was so jam-packed with random titbits I didn't know where to begin, but I'll give it a go anyway.

First up, that last sign about the Battle of

Inverlochy wasn't randomly plonked in the middle of nowhere after all. It turns out that exact spot was where the Campbells finally gave up legging it from the Royalist forces. And there I was, thinking someone had just lost a map and gone rogue with a Sharpie.

Second, and I swear I am not making this up, the loch below us was said to contain a *Waterbull*. Yes, a Waterbull. Not to be confused with a bull *in* water, which is just a soggy cow. This legendary creature, clearly Nessie's slightly more bovine cousin, apparently emerges now and then to drag unsuspecting livestock into the deep. Sheep, cows, possibly the odd tourist wearing too much Gore-Tex—no one's safe. I made a mental note not to loiter near the edge.

As if a carnivorous loch-beast wasn't enough excitement for one hillside, the sign then casually dropped that this very loch—and more precisely, an island at its far end—was once home to *Macbeth*. Yes, that Macbeth. King of the Scots, haver of daggers, star of GCSE English curriculums everywhere. Not that we could see his house or anything—just a lot of mist, trees, and what might've been a duck. Still, as the sun finally started to poke its nose through the clouds, I imagined the Macbeths enjoying their lochside real estate, perhaps with Lady M nagging him about bloodstains again.

But wait, there's more. Up ahead, it declared,

we'd soon find the ruins of something called Dun Deardil—a name that sounds like it belongs in *Game of Thrones* but is in fact a *vitrified fort.* These are ancient hill forts that, for reasons nobody really understands, have at some point been *melted.* Yes, melted. Like they've been shoved in a prehistoric microwave. Apparently over 2,500 years old, these mysterious toasty ruins are found all over Scotland and Europe, and I'd always wanted to see one. Spoiler alert: they're brilliant, and also baffling.

So we carried on uphill, full of anticipation and sugar. At one point, we thought we saw people coming down towards us through the haze, but as it turned out, it was a bush. A fairly human-looking bush, but a bush nonetheless. That's the point you know your brain's getting a bit slushy and it's probably time to stop, breathe, and eat some sugar.

So we did. Chris, bless him, pulled out our very last bag of Haribos, which we inhaled with the desperate joy of people who hadn't tasted flavour in weeks. It wasn't so much eating as vacuuming. Ten seconds later, it was just an empty rustling wrapper and three grown men staring at it like it might magically refill itself.

I, however, made the rookie mistake of sitting on the grass. It *looked* dry. It *felt* dry. It was, of course, *not* dry. When I stood up a few minutes later—precisely as the midges clocked us and began circling like tiny winged sharks—I discovered that my backside was now impersonating a sponge. Drying out mid-hike is not a fast process. You might as well ask the loch to wring out your trousers for you. I really should've known better.

We trudged on and on, with the occasional grunt of a conversation just to remind ourselves we were still conscious. It became increasingly clear that we were all thoroughly, deeply, irrevocably beaten—mainly by the Devil's Staircase the day before, which had absolutely chewed us up and spat us out somewhere near Kinlochleven. Up until then, we'd had grand ideas of returning to walk the West Highland Way again, maybe even in winter so we could see the dramatic frozen north. But today, we'd officially decided to chuck that idea straight into the loch.

As we dragged ourselves forward, we stumbled into a meadow that glistened with morning dew, every blade of grass strung with spiderwebs that looked like they'd been crocheted by obsessive-compulsive arachnids. These were even better than the webs we'd seen back in Glen Orchy, and we all agreed they were beautiful—but not beautiful enough to justify the state we were currently in. "Still not worth it," I muttered to Chris, my legs barely functioning and my feet pulsing with every step like they were plotting my downfall.

Somewhere in the haze of pain, we crossed a bridge and passed a very pretty waterfall—though I only noticed this because I stopped to take a photo, and not because I was feeling particularly whimsical. No, I just desperately needed to sit down, and it turns out taking a photo is a brilliant excuse for not walking. Sadly, we were interrupted by another walker, who we asked—quite hopefully —how far we had left. He smiled (the git) and said that after the next ridge, it was downhill all the way. Which would have been great news... if the ridge hadn't looked like it was a mile away and about three hundred vertical feet above us.

With fresh despair in our bones, we shuffled on. I overtook Robin—probably out of sheer spite —and pushed on up the increasingly steep slope with Chris just ahead. Eventually, we all reached the top and, in an unusually cinematic moment, stood together gazing across what we hoped was the last big view before Fort William. It did not disappoint. The cloud had lifted just enough for us to see Ben Nevis looming to our right, and we could just about make out the winding path crawling up its side, teeming with ants that turned out to be hikers. Roughly 100,000 people make that climb every year, and judging by the trail, they'd all decided today was the day.

A sign pointed the way to Dun Deardil— our long-anticipated vitrified fort—and while Rob stayed back to rest without removing his pack (a bold move), Chris and I dumped ours and made for the summit. It started as a gentle incline but quickly escalated to "what were we thinking?" territory. Just as we were about to mutiny and turn back, we crested the hill.

Unfortunately, the fort was more *theoretical* than *visible*. There were no fiery ruins, no dramatic fused stones, just a grassy mound that looked like it had been mildly annoyed sometime around the Iron Age. The whole thing had been buried, apparently for preservation purposes, which is archaeologist-speak for "we don't want you nicking the good bits." That said, the science of these forts is still a head-scratcher. It takes temperatures of around 1,000°C to melt stone, and nobody really knows how they managed that 2,500 years ago without even the luxury of a microwave or a flamethrower. But hey—everyone loves a good unsolved mystery, right?

We rejoined Rob and admired the view into the glen below, where the road twisted and looped like it had been sketched by someone on a sugar high. Bugs Bunny himself couldn't have designed a better cartoon descent.

Then came the downhill. Oh, the joy of switching to a whole new set of muscles just as the old ones were getting the hang of things. Within minutes, my knees were screaming. Not metaphorically. I'm pretty sure I could hear them yelling profanities every time my feet hit the rough, unforgiving gravel. The track was only fit for 4x4s and sadists, and by the time we hit the lower stretch, my feet had joined the chorus of complaints.

Relief came in the form of a chat with two women heading up the way we'd come. They were regulars on this route and seemed far too cheerful for my liking. They had a lovely labrador with them, though "lovely" might be generous—he was friendly, yes, but also determined to become more intimately acquainted with me than I was comfortable with. He zigzagged through our legs, darted into the trees like he'd just seen a ghost, and returned seconds later for more awkward sniffing. I never did find out what he was chasing, but if it was dignity, I can confirm there was none left to catch.

Although the day had turned into quite a stunner, with proper sunshine replacing the damp gloom we'd started with, we were still mildly alarmed to hear that the two ladies we'd met were heading off with nothing but a bottle of water and zero waterproofs between them. I involuntarily shuddered as my brain revisited that soul-destroying first day from Milngavie to Drymen, where it rained sideways, upside down and possibly from beneath for ten straight hours. We'd very nearly packed it all in before we'd even got going. To make matters worse, one of the women was wearing jeans, which are fine for shopping or dinner, but in the mountains, they're like wrapping your legs in a sponge. Brave? Possibly. Stupid? Also possible. Only they would know for sure—when, and if, they stumbled soggily into Kinlochleven.

We wished them luck and shuffled onward, beginning the long, limping descent into Glen Nevis. Below us, tiny houses dotted the valley floor like Monopoly pieces, and we could clearly make out the campsite, which, in its lush green rectangle of hope, gleamed like paradise itself.

Normally, downhill means faster. Not today. Today, our legs had clearly signed a petition and gone on strike. We stopped more times than a learner driver in a roundabout, and at one point, the path had the absolute gall to go *uphill* again. At this stage. Rude.

After what felt like the descent of a lifetime—and possibly was—we finally emerged onto tarmac at the bottom of the glen, and there it was: Fort William! Or at least the outskirts of it. Turns out, we still had a couple of miles to go, which felt like a personal insult. But every heavy-footed step dragged us closer to glory. And let me tell you, that last two miles might as well have been ten.

Arriving in Fort William was... weird. There was no welcoming banner. No raucous applause. No beaming townsfolk thrusting medals into our hands. Just traffic, tarmac, and the faint smell of chips. We wandered through the streets, a little dazed, and passed what used to be the *original* finishing point of the West Highland Way. We took a photo there, partly for nostalgia and partly because we weren't entirely sure where the *new* finish actually was.

Ah yes, the cunning powers-that-be had shifted the official end of the trail right into the middle of town, presumably so hikers would stagger straight past every shop, café, and "Wee Dram" whisky bar en route to the finish. Capitalism at its finest.

Soon, we were marching three abreast down Fort William's high street, parting the crowds like Moses through the Red Sea. It might have been out of admiration. It might have been our stench. Either way, it worked. In my head, we looked like slow-mo heroes from an Oscar-winning epic. In reality, we were more like the Three Stooges in hiking boots.

We passed Greggs, Superdrug, a small dog in a rucksack, and a man arguing with a seagull, before we finally reached what we *thought* was the end. It wasn't. It was a kebab shop. The disappointment was real.

But then—there it was. The real finish line. The actual end of the West Highland Way. A small bench with a statue of a man massaging his feet like they'd personally offended him. At first, we tried to figure out who this sore-footed hero might be—Tom Weir? John Muir? Some other semi-mystical Scottish wanderer from history?

Nope. Just a bloke with sore feet. Literally. The statue is called *Man with Sore Feet*, created by David Annand, and it marks the official end of the route since 2010. A bit of an anti-climax, really. Not a fanfare or a complimentary dram in sight. Before that, the end had been back near the Edinburgh Woollen Mill on the outskirts of town, where weary hikers used to stop for certificates, novelty t-shirts, and the essential rubber-stamping of their West Highland Way passports. I suspect the shop's revenue halved overnight.

Still, we made it. A hundred miles through moors and midges, past bothies and bogs, up staircases built by Satan himself, and over mountains that laughed in our sweaty faces. And now, all that was left to do... was sit on a bench with a man who understood our pain.

The only thing he was missing was the bottle of ibuprofen.

Moving the end of the route probably cheered up the owners of the Wetherspoon's pub, though, which was now perfectly plonked next to the smelly-footed statue and, quite fittingly, called *The Great Glen*. It was ideally positioned to catch every sweaty, starving hiker stumbling across the finish line, which is precisely where we went next. Or rather, where we *tried* to go next.

We were greeted at the door by a young woman who winced as if she'd just caught a whiff of a compost heap. When we asked if there was a table, she told us they were fully booked... *for the rest of the year*. Now, I'm not saying we were at our most dazzling and groomed, but come on—we'd just walked a hundred miles. A bit of stubble and some eau de soggy socks should have been expected.

Chris, bless him, now bore an uncanny resemblance to Tom Hanks—though not the well-dressed, motivational version from *Forrest Gump*. No, this was more *Castaway*, day 743, complete with vacant eyes and the wild look of a man who's had long conversations with inanimate objects. As for me, I was teetering on the visual spectrum between "rugged adventurer" and "unhoused rascal." And Rob? He just looked like a freshly escaped convict with a grudge against society.

Regardless, we were turned away. I blamed COVID restrictions. Or possibly our faces. Either way, we left, thanking her for her service, even though she'd been about as useful as a solar-powered torch in a blackout. I caught the end of her final sentence, but it came out as "blah, blah, blah," and frankly, I was too tired and petty to pretend otherwise. Sometimes I think I should try to be a nicer person. Then I laugh and carry on being me.

So, back to the bench we went—our new spiritual home—and claimed a patch of grass like kings. Rob fetched food, Chris fetched drinks, and before long, we were dining like royalty on roast pork sandwiches and a bottle of Coke, which was probably better than whatever microwave lasagne Wetherspoon's would've scraped together anyway.

As we lounged, the ladies drove by and beeped the horn at *exactly* the right moment. Almost cinematic. They soon found us, presumably by following the trail of mud and the smell, and we hobbled back to the car like returning war veterans. While we flopped into the boot, they went shopping and returned triumphantly an hour later with bags full of tat that looked fantastic *because* they were still on holiday.

Back in Drymen and finally showered and shaved, I switched on the TV for the first time in a week... and promptly switched it off again. The news always starts with "Good evening" before spending the next 30 minutes explaining why it definitely isn't.

We wandered outside and were treated to the sound of a lone piper on the village green, which was weirdly emotional. I told my son bagpipes were invented in Egypt and brought to Scotland by the Romans. He told me I was an idiot. He may be right, but I am *an educated* idiot.

When the piper packed up his dead cat and left, I fired up the drone for one last flight, this time over Buchanan Castle. It was all turrets and towers peeking out from a sea of green—like nature was slowly reclaiming it, vine by vine. The castle, once built for the Duke of Montrose (not the one Rob Roy had a kerfuffle with, but a much later one), had been turned into a hospital during World War II and even briefly housed one Rudolf Hess after he parachuted into Scotland in a half-baked attempt to negotiate peace. He failed, obviously, and eventually died in Spandau Prison aged 93, which was probably still less uncomfortable than walking the West Highland Way.

Rob admired my drone skills until I let Chris have a go. Hovering it just above Rob's shiny dome, I explained how the drone had obstacle detection and would stop before hitting anything. "It's foolproof," I said. "Go on, fly it straight at him."

Chris did. Slowly. Very slowly.

It didn't stop.

The drone clattered off Rob's cranium like a pissed wasp hitting a window, before spiralling to the ground in a dramatic, high-pitched tantrum. Thankfully, the drone was fine. Rob was not. We patched his head up with a plaster and told him he was lucky—it's not like he uses what's *in* his head anyway.

Drone tucked safely away, we headed to the Clachan for a well-earned pint. We were joined by Frances from Kip in the Kirk, the very woman who'd saved our hike back when we were half-drowned and ready to quit. We promised to tell everyone about her brilliant hostel. Without her, we wouldn't have finished the walk. In fact, we might have died somewhere near a fence post in Drymen.

She told us the pub's first landlady was Rob Roy's sister—Mistress Gow—which is why the Rob Roy Way starts just outside on the village green. Billy Connolly also once lived in the village, though not at the same time, obviously.

We talked about the wild goats we'd seen by Loch Lomond. Frances asked how they smelled. "Like us," I said. "Only marginally better."

I also apologised for lighting joss sticks in her bathroom. Frances looked puzzled and said, "We don't *have* any joss sticks." "Exactly," I said.

Then came the haggis. Yes, the real stuff—not the mythical furry creature with uneven legs. It's like crumbly sausage, made of sheep heart, lungs and liver, all minced with onions, suet and spice, then traditionally stuffed inside a sheep's stomach. Doesn't *sound* appealing, but let me tell you—it's absolutely delicious. I don't care what's in it. I'd eat it again tomorrow.

We reminisced about the walk, the freakishly good weather, the quarter-million steps, the fact that we'd somehow escaped the week without a single blister. We joked that it had taken us three months to complete the trail, though in reality, we'd only walked for six days. Six days of sweat, suffering, stupidity and scenery so good it made your soul ache.

And when I looked across at Rob and Chris, I was quietly grateful. Not just for the laughs, or the whisky-laced coffees, or the drone-headbutting incidents, but because back when I thought the walk was over—when my shin screamed out and my mood nosedived—they hadn't left me behind. They'd waited. Because that's what mates do.

And that's how we all ended up here. Full of haggis. Full of stories. Full of aches and blisters and memories.

And full of beer.

Conclusion

From the moment we set off, so long ago and so far away in the exotic lands of Milngavie, it felt like this finish line might never come. What began as a simple idea—three mates walking a trail together—turned into an odyssey stretched across seasons, injury, family chaos, and work commitments. There was a point, somewhere between Drymen and despair, where it felt like we might never finish this thing at all.

And yet—miraculously—my early prediction that we'd probably wrap it up by September, made during one of Chris's three-hour photo sessions on Day One, turned out to be surprisingly accurate. Not because of the photography, mind you, but because my leg decided to betray me like a medieval courtier with a grudge.

Still, we made it. We took everything this trail hurled at us—rain, wind, midges, mud, drama, emotional meltdowns, and questionable food—and we walked every single mile. It might not be the longest walk in the world, or the toughest, but it was a challenge to *us*—three ordinary blokes with an extraordinary fondness for mountains and masochism.

Yes, it was hard. Yes, we whinged. Yes, there were definitely moments when each of us mentally buried the others somewhere near a scenic waterfall. But we kept going. We encouraged each other. We waited when one of us faltered. We stuck it out. And in doing so, we finished what we started.

We learned a few things, too. For starters, no amount of preparation guarantees success. You can have all the gear and a colour-coded spreadsheet, and your shin will still blow out on Day One if it feels like it. Also, while it's important to keep an eye on your footing to avoid tripping over a rock or an overconfident frog, it's just as important to stop. Look around. Take it all in. And for the love of all things Scottish, remember to look *behind* you occasionally. Some of the best views are there—quiet, unexpected, and waiting.

Oh, and one last thing: trail mileage is a work of fiction. Just because a guidebook says it's 15 miles doesn't mean it won't *feel* like 27. Especially the last few. They are always the hardest. But somehow, they are also the most rewarding.

So... what's next?

Well. You'll just have to wait and see.

Afterword

Thanks for reading Northbound on the West Highland Way!

I hope you enjoyed the chaos, midges, and borderline bad decisions as much as I enjoyed walking through them and writing it all down so you didn't have to.

If you've got a minute (and still have feeling in your thumbs), I'd really appreciate an honest review. Reviews help authors like me spread the word - and trust me, shouting into the void only gets you so far.

And if you made it to the end without running for the hills (or even if you did), feel free to check out one of my other books. If this one didn't put you off entirely, there's a good chance you'll enjoy those too.

Books By This Author

Coast To Coast Path: Finding Wainwright's England

Offa's Dyke Path: Lost In The Woods

54 Degrees North

Coastal Capers: Walking The Yorkshire Coast Path

Rambling On: Lost On The Cleveland Way

Hadrian's Wall Path

Southbound On The Viking Way

All Hills High And Low: The Herriot Way

A Walk On The Wild Side: The Yorkshire Wolds Way

One Step At A Time: The Wilberforce Way

Printed in Dunstable, United Kingdom